THE DUALITY OF BEING

PERSPECTIVES FROM
MULTIDIMENSIONAL TRAVEL

SUSAN NICHOLAS, MD

Grateful acknowledgment is made for permission to reproduce the poem "Incremental" by John Dalton, M.D. Copyright ©1993 by John Dalton. Used by permission of the author.

Copyright © 2018 by Susan Nicholas, M.D. All rights reserved. No part of this publication may be reproduced or transmitted in any form or by any means, mechanical or electronic, including photocopying and recording, or by any information storage and retrieval system, without permission in writing from the publisher (except by a reviewer, who may quote brief passages in a review). For permission, contact ContactUs@SusanNicholas.org.

Human Consciousness Consortium
Atlanta, Georgia 30339
Website: www.SusanNicholas.org
Email: ConsciousBooks@SusanNicholas.org

ISBN 978-1-7324336-0-1 (print)
ISBN 978-1-7324336-2-5 (ebook)

Library of Congress Control Number 2018907633

For Michelle and Ninfa

CONTENTS

Introduction 9
The Duality of Being

PART ONE 19
Transcending the Third Dimension

    Chapter 1 22
    First Flight

    Chapter 2 24
    Near-Earth Dimensions

    Chapter 3 36
    The True Self

    Chapter 4 45
    The Ascension Process

    Chapter 5 55
    Elevating Your Frequency

    Chapter 6 72
    Being Quiet

Chapter 7 81
Sleep and Rest

Chapter 8 86
Balance

Chapter 9 93
A Circuitous Path

Chapter 10 102
The Root of Happiness

PART TWO 105
Human Constructs to Transcend

Chapter 11 108
Time

Chapter 12 113
Money

Chapter 13 134
Race

Chapter 14 142
Religion

PART THREE 151
Perspective on Life after Multidimensional Travel

Chapter 15. 155
Authenticity

Chapter 16. 160
Relationships

Chapter 17. 171
Love, Sex, and Intimacy

Chapter 18. 177
Gender and the Energy Body

Chapter 19. 181
Children

Chapter 20 190
Powers

Chapter 21. 195
Thoughts

Chapter 22 201
The Future

Chapter 23 207
Sentience

Chapter 24 212
Earth's Energy

Chapter 25 217
Purpose

Chapter 26 222
Death

Acknowledgments. 230

Notes 232

Resources. .234

About the Author 235

INTRODUCTION
The Duality of Being

Each of us has the innate ability to separate our life energy from our physical body and travel into faraway dimensions. Although we do not fully understand the mechanisms, we know from anecdotal reports that the energy body has an infinite capacity to travel to dimensions far beyond ours without bringing harm or death to the physical body. Many who have experienced multidimensional travel have had a near-death experience that led to this life-changing phenomenon or what has been termed a *crisis awakening*. Though this type of energetic travel cannot be measured or assessed with current scientific tools, it is as real an experience as traveling by airplane to visit coveted locations around the world. Higher consciousness lies in the metaphysical realms today only because it is not fully understood or accepted by the people of our civilization and age. Multidimensional travel nonetheless, offers us a gateway to higher and expanded levels of consciousness.

Multidimensional travel is experienced by the individuals who resonate with it, and who possess the health and energetic frequency to endure a temporary separation from the body. It is an intensely personal experience that can occur during times of deep introspection and longing for truth. If my own experience is a reasonable indication, conscious multidimensional travel can shape our perspectives on broader aspects of human existence. In writing this book, *The Duality of Being*, I aim to pass on to you some of the discoveries I made while my energy body was journeying.

In 2012, I had a conscious awakening and developed the ability to travel out of my body and into far dimensions spontaneously. My awakening occurred during a time in my life of profound sadness that served as a lifting off point. Multidimensional out-of-body travel has been the most awe-inspiring experience of my life. I anticipate this phenomenon to be the penultimate experience of my embodied existence—the *ultimate* experience being my physical death—as my soul has heard *l'appel du vide*, the "call of the void."

The Duality of Being details my life and the convoluted journey I made into higher realms of consciousness through my out-of-body travels. In it, I will share with you the perspectives I've gained that have improved my quality of life, decisions, and relationships. The world we share appears simpler through the eyes of multidimensional travelers akin to myself. Experiencing true consciousness allows me to handle life with a sense of inner calm and understanding. It is only through consciousness that I have achieved inner happiness and a clear sense of well-being. I hope that many of my insights will be similarly valuable and enlightening for you. *True* consciousness is consciousness from the perspective of the soul. Real consciousness is not waking up each day to the physical reality you have created for yourself. Actual consciousness comes from the expanded awareness that you are infinitely more than your physical body and that reality is a concept far beyond our physical world.

Consciousness is not something to be measured but rather to be experienced. To be consciously aware is not something that is learned, it is something that you *are*. It is a manner of being. Conscious awareness does not require you to follow any guru or religious text. It does not require or request for you to go to a mountaintop, to fast, or to otherwise isolate yourself from life. Consciousness requires no tithing, and you are the master.

Higher consciousness is neither an intellectual pursuit nor can its development be taught like a physical skill or subject in school. It is an intrinsic aspect of your being that must be awakened. It is something that is felt deep within. Accessing higher realms of consciousness requires the process of introspection and is a journey taken over many lifetimes.

We can never reach the finish line on the path to conscious awareness as we are ever-evolving beings. The journey is as individual as each person who explores his or her own worldly life experience. As each life path on Earth is unique, so too is our consciousness.

In this book, I can only share my personal experience with higher frequencies of awareness. In doing so, I reassure you that it is possible for you to elevate your frequency as well. Out-of-body, multidimensional travel is available to you should you desire it, but please understand that it is just one of many access points to higher consciousness and alternate dimensions of reality. The journey of awakening your consciousness will be yours, just as the life you lead on Earth is expressly yours. No two embodied souls could have an identical enlightened experience. Your consciousness is for you to unveil.

Similarly, no two individuals awaken in precisely the same way. Though the revelations of your awakening process will be personal, other conscious beings are willing and waiting to assist you in making sense of it, helping you to ease any fears, should they arise. Both earthbound guides, such as myself, and ethereal guides may assist you at various points on your path of spiritual development, but please understand that it is you who must walk the way. A genuinely conscious being may help you to reach the access point into altered states of consciousness and energy travel, but the journey thereafter belongs to you.

Consciousness does not insist upon hours of meditation or other physical practices. Once you can quiet your mind enough to hear your inner voice, you can begin to access this sacred aspect of your being. The wondrous experiences that higher consciousness delivers to you from that point onward will be yours alone to experience.

Please note that there is a distinction to be made between hearing your inner voice and *listening* to it. Imagine hearing the television running in the background as you do your household chores. You can hear the TV, but are you really listening to it? Listening has become a lost virtue in our busy lives and it is harder still in the conscious realm. Listening to your inner voice requires attention.

Listening also demands action. Once you begin to listen to your higher self, you will realize that it has been telling you to do something long overdue. If you are interested in having similar experiences to the ones that I describe in these pages, you must listen and act. The actions required to propel you into conscious awareness will be revealed to you, and you will soon come to realize you already knew what you had to do. All the answers have always been within you.

Reading this book may be the first of a thousand steps you take toward your conscious awakening.

Elevating your consciousness is the byproduct of connecting with your higher self, which is the aspect of your being that is connected to the Source energy of the Universe. To experience higher consciousness involves allowing your body to rest peacefully while your energy body "wakes up" inside you. This awakened energy body will serve as the portal to your dual existence. Some people refer to this energy body as the *soul*. It is the part of you that is eternally connected to the Source energy and thereby all of humanity. It is through its aegis that the veil of consciousness is lifted.

Once awakened, the experience of being conscious explains itself. Any being who is truly conscious will not question the existence of consciousness or attempt to use physical instruments to prove it because it is neither necessary nor possible. Consciousness cannot be proved any more than the feeling of true love can. It just is, as anyone who has experienced love can attest. Similarly, consciousness cannot be found in the gray or white matter of the physical brain. Nor does it have a subcellular basis in our neurons. The brain is designed to be in service to the physical body. Consciousness, on the other hand, resides in a nonphysical state. Understanding consciousness is not something one learns or studies. It does not reside within the boundaries of science or medicine. It is a discovery made only from within.

No religion can bring you closer to your inner consciousness. It is only from seeking the truth inside yourself that your individual consciousness can be revealed. The fact of the matter is that consciousness is an introspective journey that occurs over many lifetimes. Some of these lifetimes are spent on Earth, whereas others may be spent elsewhere.

Waking up during the current Earth age is not an experience all living beings will have. The acknowledgment of a greater continuum of existence won't resonate with all beings on the planet in the present millennium. The call to consciousness will resonate only with those who are ready.

Planet Earth is entering a new era where the pace of the development of higher awareness among its inhabitants is accelerating. The acceleration means that more embodied souls will seek and experience some aspect of awakening before their physical death. You will be able to recognize such beings because they will have no fear at the time of their final passing. Instead, they will exude a calm knowingness, an innate understanding. The whole point of becoming consciously aware is to ease your transition out of Earth's third dimension into a higher frequency when you die. The idea, or purpose, if we can call it that, is to elevate your frequency while still on Earth, so you do not carry over dense energy at that time, preventing your ascension to the highest possible dimension you can reach.

We tend to fear death because its nature remains unknown to most of us. However, once we become familiar with and comfortable about what is on the other side of this life experience, the death of our physical form will no longer provoke the same heavy wariness from us that it had in the past. Conscious awareness allows the gravity of death to be lifted. We can feel genuinely happy and show our respect for the life we've experienced and the challenges we've overcome. Each life lesson earnestly learned moves us closer to attunement with the flight-enabling frequency.

Death of the physical body is one of many illusions of the third dimension. The energy body exists in an embodiment (for example, your physical body or my physical body) so it may mature in certain ways. When the energy body has evolved sufficiently, or as much as it can during a single incarnation, it sheds the human shell and moves on to another enriching experience. It is important to know that shedding the body is nothing to fear. It is the struggle to hold on to the body that creates so much pain. Rest assured that letting go is the easy part.

We assign a lot of meaning to physical death because we do not see it for what it is. Death is a transition, the commencement of yet another phase of existence. Death is to be revered as it essentially represents graduation from one experience and the beginning of another. Finding peace in letting go of the body is understanding that there is infinitely more to experience outside of the confines of Earth.

Being prepared for your final transition off the planet is paramount. The vibrational frequency at final separation helps to define where you land on the "other side" of this life. Make every effort to release as much dense energy as possible, so that when you do transition you are full of love and light. There exist other incarnations that are not as arduous or heavy as this one. There is the opportunity to exist in a light body that enables travel to multiple dimensions. Imagine the experiences you could have exploring the cosmos, meeting new forms of life energy, and rejoining with your various legacy soul groups. Imagine the life you would like to create for yourself, and you can have it. The key is to get out of your own way.

The energetic frequency at which you are vibrating is very important both on and off the planet. Living at higher and higher frequencies allows for ascension at death, as I've said, but it also brings with it ease during life. The *letting go* of which I have been speaking involves the release of dense thoughts and feelings, such as fears and grievances, as well as the detachment from physical things. When you no longer take things personally and allow your feelings to be acknowledged and then released, you will find life to be much more pleasant. (I know, this is easier said than done. We will explore the topic of *letting go* throughout the book.)

Things can be nice to have. Appreciate and enjoy them. However, when the time comes, be free to release all physical things too.

What you are left with after letting go of everything is peace of mind, body, and spirit. Being peaceful does not mean you stop trying or achieving. It means you do all that you can do and release the rest to the Universe. Trust that what you need will show up for you in ways that are perhaps even better than you could have imagined. The Universe wants to serve you. Acknowledge the love and power of the Source of all life. Allow yourself to return to oneness with all that *is*.

As you move to a higher frequency by releasing your heavy baggage, you can expect a sincere reverence for the Earth to emerge. You will find love and understanding for all living things and recognize the Earth's energy as supreme and awe-inspiring. The Earth is always in motion, working to elevate the frequency of its own vibration. By elevating your frequency, you, in turn, assist the Earth on its journey because you are a part of the Earth. Know that the Earth also is learning and evolving. You mustn't forget that each human has a role to play in the planet's evolution.

The planet has taken many eons to arrive where it is today. It has sustained much life through cosmic cycles dating back billions of years. There were more enlightened beings in past Earth cycles than there are today. It is feasible that Earth will again have a greater number of conscious beings inhabiting it, people who will have greater respect for it and all the life it supports. The Earth needs each of us to elevate our vibrational frequency to achieve this aim because, in doing so, we grow more respectful of the planet. Our emotional maturity goes a long way in helping the planet achieve its own ascension.

Once you have elevated your frequency sufficiently to enable soul travel, you will find that conscious multidimensional travel allows you to see people for who they really are, without the burdens they carry in their lives. Because of soul flight, you will come to see the true beauty and love that resonates within all of us. The pureness of love becomes visible. It is only with the heart that we can see rightly. It's only with the heart that we can see inner light. What I mean is that the subjective physical eye does not see the light in the being. Soul light, which is nonphysical, resonates on the heart level.

I am overwhelmed with gratitude and peace within to have had the extraordinary opportunity to take flight while still alive in a human body. I am sharing my experience in this book so that anyone who reads my message will no longer be afraid of physical death. In a manner of speaking, I have "died" a thousand deaths and can now come to you with a description of my journeys into levels of consciousness and frequencies that lie beyond the third dimension we share here on Earth. You may have similar experiences or wildly different ones when you travel out of the body. There is no right or wrong. We each experience travel that is consistent with our frequency and the immediate capacity of our consciousness.

Some people will experience near-Earth dimensions that have religious contexts or other familiar scenes that bring them comfort. Other dimensions experienced may have no earthly counterparts. Most people who engage in conscious soul flight have conscious experiences in their light bodies, particularly at first, while some people transcend Earth's framework entirely and travel as mere points of light right from the start. As you begin your explorations, please remember that you are not in a competition or a race. There are a multitude of paths to higher consciousness, and all paths ultimately lead to eternity. Conscious soul travel out of body is not all there is to conscious awareness. Even if you never consciously travel, do the introspective work to elevate your frequency so that you are ready for the moment of your final transition out of body.

Having made many journeys into multiple dimensions, I now know that this journey to Earth as a physical human being will be my last incarnation in the third dimension. It has been an extraordinary experience.

PART ONE

Transcending the Third Dimension

In Part One, I will share the details of my early out-of-body experiences: how I came to leave my body, what it feels like to leave it, and the fundamental things I learned about how we can move around when we are disencumbered. Much of my early dimensional travel was experienced in what I refer to as my *light* body.

Some readers may recognize this type of light-body, multidimensional travel as the activation of the sacred geometry of the Merkabah. *Merkabah* is a Hebrew term combining the three roots *mer*—meaning "light," *ka*—meaning "spirit," and *bah*—meaning "body." It is important to note that I did not purposefully activate my Merkabah, as I was unaware of its existence at the time. My experience with multidimensional travel was unexpected and to my knowledge, spontaneous, and thereby, I expect the same is available to everyone.

To maintain the ability to travel into multiple dimensions, the body must undergo changes toward optimal health and balance. Part One will reveal the changes I underwent and how I achieved the balance in my body and in life as whole to sustain soul travel for many years. As you shall see, soul flight is not fearsome; it is a freeing and most fascinating passage into conscious awareness.

CHAPTER 1

First Flight

In 2012, I found myself deeply unhappy. I was in an unfulfilling relationship with a philandering partner who did not know how to love me. I had a beautiful toddler who demanded everything of me. I was running my own start-up company and getting nowhere it seemed. I had always been thin and attractive. But now I hated to look at myself or to be photographed because I felt miserable and exhausted most of the time. I had developed a herniated disc in my lower back which was causing me so much pain that at times I was unable to walk. What was left of my self-esteem was sinking in a deepening pool of despair. I felt diminished, unheard, and bereaved at the loss of the person I had been.

How did I get here? I thought. I was a doctor, an entrepreneur, and a good mother. I was also a very sad person who no longer wished to be alive.

When I lay down to sleep at night, I would plead with myself to go home. I did not know where or what "home" actually was, but I begged to go there anyway. I would cry for no apparent reason, while watching a movie, lying in bed, or taking a shower. I was overwhelmed with a visceral kind of sadness that nothing could touch. The feeling inside of me felt like an ever-deepening emptiness, a void.

My thoughts of inconsolable grief were continually running in the background like a machine. The amplitude of persistent noise in my mind reminded me of a humming generator, its intrusion only fully noticed once it shuts off. I had a constant dialogue in my head about what was wrong with me, what the meaning of my life was, and why I was here.

Then one night, I "dreamed" that I was soaring high in the night sky above a big city full of lights. I felt so light and peaceful that I couldn't believe it. I had never flown in a dream before—not like this. A voice beside me sensed my awareness of the experience's newness and told me not to look down. Naturally, I looked down straight away only to find the city beneath me had turned to crumbling ash. I realized that what I had been seeing wasn't a city at all, only an illusion created to pacify my immature mind. I wasn't flying in the typical sense either.

Upon my spontaneous recognition of this reality, I suddenly became conscious of my soul's true nature for a moment. With that glimpse, I realized I did not have a body and was no longer on Earth—and that I wasn't dreaming! I instinctively understood that I was existing as pure energy.

And I was immediately overcome with fear.

In an instant, I found myself back in my bed and inside of my body. I lay there wide-awake promising myself that if I ever had the chance to fly again, I would not be afraid.

That night flight marked the beginning of my conscious awakening.

CHAPTER 2
Near-Earth Dimensions

In the early hours of the morning following my first soul flight, I reflected upon how the experience I'd had was not a typical dream. A few days later, I began asking around to see if any of my friends had ever had a similar experience. I asked person after person—and none had a clue what I was describing. I suspected that I'd had an out-of-body experience (OBE). Because I had only heard of OBEs related to near-death experiences at that point, I wondered if this OBE was a sign that my life was nearing its end.

My earliest OBEs took place in what I can only describe as near-Earth dimensions. Near-Earth dimensions closely resemble our Earth's environment but have different frequencies. Earth exists today in a dense, physical state that we term the third dimension; or put another way, we inhabit Earth 3.0. A near-Earth dimension could be described as Earth 2.9 or even Earth 3.1, somewhere where the experience of that dimension is like being on Earth but slightly more or less dense.

There is an inverse relationship between energetic frequency and density. The higher the frequency, the less dense or physical the dimension. The lower the frequency, the denser it is. The density (physicality) of a dimension, however, does not make it more real or less real to experience. In every other respect than this, near-Earth dimensions are no different than what we perceive as reality here on Earth. The experience only differs because we are visiting these places as beings of energy rather than as embodied human beings.

Just as there are multiple realities on Earth 3.0, each dimension within itself has a multitude of created realities. In our world, a person living in a penthouse apartment in Manhattan experiences reality differently than a person leading a nomadic lifestyle in a yurt in the Gobi Desert. Both existences are real and belong to Earth 3.0, but they differ widely. In the same way that we can experience multiple realities in the third dimension, we also can have a variety of different experiences in any other dimension we visit when we are out of the body.

The physical human body is designed specifically for the third-dimensional Earth environment. To experience higher or lower energetic frequencies, we must leave the physical body behind and in doing so travel in the *energy body* or *finer body*. The finer body is known to many people as the *light body*, and it is one of the few means by which we can travel to different dimensions. It is referred to as *light* because it is not heavy like the physical body, rather than because it is illuminated. Every person has a light body, yet few of us are conscious of its existence.

Multidimensional travel takes you to energetic frequencies, as opposed to physical places or geographies. At varying frequencies, certain types of energetic beings exist who interact with Earth-like objects. For example, at frequency Earth 3.1, you might encounter what appears to be human beings engaged in activities that are routine and familiar, like eating and drinking or walking and talking.

During my travels, I have learned that many people who die and depart Earth will exist in a near-Earth dimension for a period. The less dense near-Earth dimensions allow these souls to relax and heal before they reincarnate into another dense, physical body. Some souls remain in energetic form and move on to other dimensions after this period rather than reincarnating.

On my conscious path, I began having scores of OBEs, not only at night but in the middle of the day. A thick tiredness would come over me, sending me for a nap. Like a flash, I was "out." It felt like energy waves flowing inside of me were escaping through my hands and feet. I was literally slipping out of my physical body, which would shudder from the sheer speed of the energy flow. These were my first conscious experiences of separating my energy self from my physical self. Until then, I had never thought of myself as a being of pure energy before.

I began writing about these experiences and sketching pictures of what I saw when I was out of my body. I didn't have the precise words yet to describe my experiences except to say that they were *surreal* and *unearthly*. I began scouring the internet looking for anything that would help me to explain my experiences, but I found very little beyond anecdotal astral travel commentary.

As a physician, I wondered if there was a physical rationale for what I was seeing. I thought maybe I had a brain tumor or something, and that this condition would prove fatal. I remember how I even warned my partner, "If I go out again, I might not come back." Hearing this, he got angry with me and asked me if I believed he didn't need me or that our son didn't need a mother.

I was enjoying my OBEs and learning so much about myself. I knew the travels weren't about deserting my son per se, but I did feel conflicted about the prospect of leaving him if I were to die. I had no intention of abandoning my family, but I did sense that the pull to leave my body was beyond my choice, that I could not resist it.

The forces I encountered during my early flights were so powerful and liberating that returning to my body and its physical reality brought me the utmost displeasure. Experiencing the perfection of my light body and higher dimensions made the imperfections of my physical life almost unbearable. Even so, when I returned from traveling, I began to perceive life on Earth very differently.

In one memorable OBE, I arrived outside a familiar type of meeting place one evening in a faraway dimension. It looked like a cathedral of some sort, with tall wooden doors that at the same time appeared translucent and ethereal. The doors were ajar, and I could hear what sounded like hundreds of muted voices on the inside. As I approached, an astonished female voice asked me, "How did you get here?" I replied that I didn't know, that I had just arrived.

Through the delusive crack of the door, I could see points of light, like candles, burning behind a gossamer shade. It felt like I belonged there, so I moved forward to pass through the doors. The voice stopped me with its energy, saying that I could not go in yet, but I didn't want to listen. I was drawn to this place as if I knew the people inside. Ignoring the instructions, I hastily approached the doors again, wanting to see for myself what was going on inside.

Just like that, I was sent back to my body.

After this particular soul flight, I understood that I was not dying but traveling. Of course, I could always decide to take my own life, but choosing to stay out of my body permanently was not a decision I could make while journeying. I was forty years old at the time, and other than the sadness I was carrying I was healthy.

When I traveled, I did not have a body—or at least not one that I could see—and I did not encounter other people per se. I would feel the energy of other beings and they could feel mine. We communicated telepathically.

When you travel as pure energy, you see although you don't have eyes. You also hear without ears and feel without touch. I was never alone, and I was never afraid. It all seemed very natural. Traveling to other dimensions was never scary to me, just different—but in a familiar kind of way. I even seemed to know my way around a multitude of dimensions.

Interestingly, whenever I am leaving my body, it feels like I am falling, not rising. If you can imagine the feeling in your body of falling into the deepest, bottomless abyss you could imagine, that's how it feels. Like falling in complete darkness at the speed of light. Beyond any rational notion, I began to welcome this sensation because when I was out, I felt incredibly free.

Initially, taking trips such as these is hard on the body and the psyche. Your physical human body must attune to the energetic frequency of multidimensional travel. I came to learn that the difficulty of the initial journeys came from escaping Earth's dense time construct. Time is a force to be reckoned with. Facing the challenges of the first journey, I suspect, is why many people who have had one OBE never wish to repeat it, or at the very least, become paralyzed with fear.

Challenges notwithstanding, I became a frequent flyer. I would often leave my body in the middle of the night, usually during my second interval of deep sleep in the hours between 2 am and 4 am. I would travel so fast that my physical body would shudder while I was traveling, and I would wake up in a pool of sweat, dampened to the point that I would have to change my clothes upon my return.

I didn't know it then, but in those early travels I was remembering myself as a connected energy being.

Despite the surreal nature of my early soul-journeying experiences, I was not exactly sure what was going on. Being a rational person, during the day I would conduct research to make sense of this phenomenon. Among other literature I read were a couple of titles by Robert Monroe, founder of the Monroe Institute in Virginia, who died in 1995 after decades of traveling out of body. From his descriptions, his experiences when out of body seemed closest to mine. However, his methods for detaching his energy body from his physical body were different than mine.

I decided to attend the Monroe Institute's Out-of-Body Intensive course after I had already documented approximately eighteen distinct types of out-of-body experiences on my own. I did not know how I was doing it, but for me, the travel was spontaneous and effortless.

At the time, I was interested in learning more about the phenomenon of being a multidimensional traveler, meeting like-minded individuals, and having more control over the travel, like Mr. Monroe. Although I didn't find what I was looking for at the Institute, I met several other individuals who, like me, were experimenting with regular OBE travel.

Interestingly, the intensive course teaches its students to get out of body using sound in what I term a *heavy body*, doing what I think of as "local" travel around their houses or neighborhoods. Traveling out of body can take several forms. Traveling in a heavy body is like being a slightly altered version of yourself interacting with a slightly altered Earth environment. You still recognize yourself. Many people refer to this form of travel as *lucid dreaming*.

The difference between a heavy body and a light body is in the frequency. When traveling in a heavy body, for example, you might feel like you are moving in slow motion, having to propel yourself through the air. It feels exhausting, as if every movement requires extraordinary effort. With this type of travel, individuals may experience getting stuck in the ceiling or between walls.

Heavy-body travel feels as if it exists in a dimension even denser and more material than our third dimension. Let's call it Earth 2.9.

I did not like the sensation of being heavy when out of my body or staying close to home, as my personal experiences with flight before then were light, fascinating, and far reaching. I had already traveled throughout the cosmos.

It wasn't just me who felt that heavy-body travel was a cumbersome form of travel. No one else I encountered who was doing out-of-body exploration traveled spontaneously in the way that I did. Most found it awkward to get out of body. That said, they seemed to enjoy the experience once they succeeded.

At the Monroe Institute, I was introduced to Reiki therapy and the energy centers in the body that are known as the *chakras*. The word *chakra* has its origin in the Sanskrit word *cakra*, meaning "wheel" or "circle." In the human body, there are seven main chakras, which are characterized by seven distinct colors and locations. While receiving my first Reiki healing session, I discovered my ability to see *auras,* the bioenergetic fields that surround all living things. I had known nothing of these things prior.

After returning home from the Monroe Institute, I decided to travel around my house using the heavy-body techniques I had learned. I managed to get out of body one evening this way and could see myself lying in my bed. For some reason, I first went into the bathroom and then headed down the main stairs. When I got to the steps, I saw my toddler son floating there, cross-legged, and asleep—also out of body. My limbs felt so heavy that I had to make a concerted effort to propel myself down the steps. It was like moving in slow motion, existing in a much denser form of gravity. I also tried to speak but could not.

Because I felt so sluggish in that realm I didn't make it very far and soon went back to my body, which displayed labored breaths reminiscent of a person with sleep apnea. I decided right then that I had no interest in traveling out again in a heavy energy body.

The one valuable insight I gained from this experience—and specifically from seeing my sleeping son floating above his body—is that we all travel out of body from time to time, although the clear majority of people are not conscious of it. As the collective human race, we are literally asleep to our higher selves!

Light-body travel occurs in slightly higher dimensions, or at higher frequencies. The word *light* in this term refers to light frequency—as in energy—but given the previous anecdote, it also references weight or density. In contrast to the heavy body, which drags you down, in your light body you feel like a younger, more energetic version of yourself. You will recognize yourself as being an idealized form of yourself from a time you felt at your best in life.

Moving around is much easier in these less dense, higher frequency realms. You yourself will create ideal images of earthly things like homes, neighborhoods, and towns with the power of your thought. Light-body travel is an ideal way to transition out of your body at death, in my view. Perhaps the ease of the transition while in a light body is a reason for the existence of such realms. Light-body experiences are more comfortable and familiar than the dimensions we can experience as points of light, for instance.

The light body is shaped like a bipedal being with two arms and two legs, much like your human body. Although it has no materiality to it, you will feel like a younger, more perfect version of yourself, and thus, you will not be shocked by your lighter existence when you first encounter it. When you are ready, you will come to recognize your true self as simply energy.

One can do all sorts of things in the light body while visiting near-Earth dimensions, like meet up with friends and have dinner parties or go ice skating. Visiting a higher frequency is like living in a fourth-dimensional earth setting. When existing in more advanced frequencies, everything is lighter, people are happier, and everything is free. You create your light-body experience in the same way you create the life you have here on Earth. Light-body dimensions have portals, as do even higher frequency dimensions, which allow for movement between dimensions. A high-frequency passage is possible, your energetic resonance permitting.

There appears to be no time in higher frequency near-Earth realms, very little gravity, and no urgency. You can eat in a light-body environment, but you do not need to. Alternate dimensions can be places of rest that are healing to the soul. Many teachers and guides are present in these dimensions because so many people have lived hard or troubled lives on Earth and thus require energetic healing and attention after they die.

You may or may not find deceased family members or friend you have known while embodied when you transition out of your body at death. You will, however, meet other life energies (souls) with similar frequencies, beliefs, and values as yours, which have been carried over from their third-dimensional lives that just ended.

One day I was having overwhelming feelings of sadness in my third-dimensional life. That night I made a soul flight in which I entered a building that reminded me of a conference center. I was in my light body and found the place filled with people walking about, talking, and standing in several lines. I arrived around the same time as several other people who were more familiar with this place than me, among them my spiritual guides. Noticing a reflection of myself in a mirror, I saw that I looked taller than normal and about twenty-five years of age. I also was thin and wore sharp-looking clothes. I felt happy and full of energy.

As I looked around me, I thought I recognized someone I knew from high school. I made a dash toward her and found myself standing in a long line. I couldn't see where the line was leading, but I thought I'd just follow those ahead of me and find out.

One of my guides noticed what I was doing and told me to get out of this line, saying that I shouldn't be there. Because I couldn't understand why not, and I wanted to see what was going on, I stayed. It was remarkable. When I got to the front of the line, I felt a strong energy pulling me forward and off my feet. An attendant readied me for a moment, and then I was sucked into a gateway. The entrance looked like a whitish, yellow light at the end of the walkway. Kind of like the long corridor you would see when boarding an airplane. In this case, the corridor was unassuming in appearance but extremely powerful in its energy. Once I had approached the threshold, there was no turning back. I was pulled in very quickly.

The journey through the portal, or corridor, was short, fast, and easy. On the other side, I immediately found myself in a new place full of people with depressed life energy—sort of like the energy I'd experienced earlier in the day—but worse. Everyone was sitting around in a crowded room with sad expressions on their faces. They also all appeared to be wearing the color gray. I felt stifled and uncomfortable and knew I had to get out of there fast. I panicked, knowing I did not belong. In that instant, my life energy returned to my physical body on Earth. Awake, I let out a huge sigh of relief, knowing that I could return to my physical existence at any moment.

As you can see from the experiences I've had, I exercise free will when I'm in other dimensions. In higher dimensions, you are given advice and guidance, but you also have the power to make your own decisions, just like you do here on Earth. Your guides are there to help you navigate this forgotten existence and yet they do not force you to evolve into a more enlightened state. You have all the time in the world, so to speak, to get things right. There is no urgency.

You see, enlightenment comes when we are ready.

I later thought back on the portal experience and realized

how important is was for me to let go of the sadness I had in me. The problem was, I wasn't exactly sure how to do that. I had carried sadness in me for so long that it had become like a permanent weight that felt intimately attached to my heart. In fact, it became a part of my personality to the point where I found it hard to smile at times. I remember graduating from medical school and despite the achievement, the sadness was there. Years later, I gave birth to a perfectly beautiful baby boy, and there it was again, like a trusted friend.

Realizing what was at stake and wanting to release sadness from my body led me to give Reiki healing a try. I did not know what to expect, but I had my first energy work performed at the Monroe Institute and it was so effective that I later trained to become a Reiki master myself.

When I signed up for my first Reiki session, I thought I was getting a special type of massage. However, when I entered the room, the healer told me not to remove my clothes and just to lie face up on the table. My mind thought, *Now, exactly how is this going to relax me?*

The practitioner began working on me, making strange sounds and waving her hands over me. I could hear her breath very distinctly. I just closed my eyes and waited. When she was finished, she sounded a bell and I woke up.

The healer said to me, "Okay, what's going on here?" and waved her hands over my chest and abdomen area. At that moment, I wept. Intuitively, I finally knew what I had to do to release myself from the sadness.

CHAPTER 3

The True Self

Most people walking the Earth today are awake but unconscious. They are awake to their immediate reality, yet unconscious to who they really are: energy beings having an embodied experience. People are known as *smart* or *ignorant, beautiful* or *ugly, good* or *bad, man* or *woman, black* or *white*, and believe that these labels somehow define them. They don't realize that the human body is only a shell, albeit a remarkable one. The life energy that inhabits the body is intimately connected to both the physical body and all that *is* in ways that can only be described as miraculous.

What is most important about the body is that it allows the true self to have a physical experience. And what is most important about the true self is invisible. The true self is pure energy having a human experience.

The outer realms have their merits and purpose, but the Earth we live on is a special and magnificent place that requires a physical form to appreciate its majesty fully. Earth is a stellar learning ground, a place to mature the soul, a place that is perhaps unique in all the Multiverse.

For most of us, the first conscious moment will occur at the time of physical death. This is the moment of imperative separation of the physical self from the energy body, as opposed to the kind of voluntary, optional out-of-body traveling we're discussing in this book. Our life energy is intimately intertwined with our human bodies. The body cannot live without it, but the inner energy is very much alive outside of the confines of the physical body.

Most people are largely unaware of the distinction between the physical self and the nonphysical self, therefore they fear physical death. This lack of awareness perpetuates our culture's exaggerated focus on youth and beauty, which arises from believing that the body is all there is. Unaware people do not understand the infinite nature of pure energy, or that it can be neither created nor destroyed.

On a few occasions out of body, I have been challenged by fearful encounters, like scenarios of being chased by ghostly wolves or slipping into widening cracks in the ground during a catastrophic earthquake. What calmed me during these experiences was remembering "I am pure energy and cannot be destroyed." Once I consciously "spoke" those words "aloud," the situation would immediately transform. The menacing wolves revealed themselves as my guides and teachers. The earthquake stopped and the ground under my feet disappeared, leaving me flying high in a sea of light, happy and full of energy.

These scenes were exercises intended to teach me, which they did. At the end of the earthquake exercise, I recall thinking that I couldn't believe I had waited so long to let go. I ran and ran in that exercise, panicked that I might fall through the rocky abyss to my death.

When experiencing portal travel, just prior to leaving my body, I would be consciously *awakened* in my sleep by a loud shift in frequency. I would hear a crack that sounded like a clap of thunder, which was loud enough to startle and awaken me inside. Otherwise, the shifts were seamless.

The usual sound of passing through a portal reminded me of the static noise made when tuning an analog radio dial. Just before you tune into a frequency, there is a distinctive crackling sound. Once I was sleeping, but awake consciously, I would cross the portal threshold into another dimension. At that point, I would receive guidance and direction from the voice I gradually began to recognize as the collective me, or my higher self. I came to understand that the full life energy that is me is so powerful that the body I am inhabiting could not possibly hold all of it. The sheer force of my full energy could disintegrate my physical self into the smallest bits of matter that are known to exist. This is a reason why we cannot take our bodies to higher frequencies. The frequency is too hard on the physical form and the journey too far.

This is true for all embodied beings. We are broken up, into a least a thousand points of light, which are scattered in different embodiments and dimensions, so we may have as many life experiences as possible. As I am writing this book, I am in female human form, living on Earth in the present era. Other parts of me are having other experiences in the Multiverse. At some point, we will all come together and form the full expression of the higher self that is *I*. Only then can the true "I" express the requisite frequency to fully reconnect with the Source energy.

In the context of consciousness, ascension is a process that wakes us up to the truth about the duality of being that characterizes our human existence. *Duality of being* is a term that describes the human condition: having both a physical and a nonphysical existence. We perceive only our physical existence as our true reality, often to the exclusion of the soul because the body that we carry is a complex, living organism that has its own mind and sensations.

When we feel pain from a physical injury, the hurt of the flesh is felt primarily by the physical body. The other aspect of our being is the soul, which is intimately connected to the body. When the physical body is injured, the energy body (soul) also has pain, but the pain is related to the emotions surrounding the situation that resulted in the injury.

For example, if we received an injury from a car crash, the energy body would feel the pain of fear and of the sorrow associated with the physical injury sustained to its connected body.

On the other hand, the mind, which is a part of the physical body, processes the feelings of the energy body and assigns meaning to them. It recounts events in a manner of endless, repetitious chatter. In the event of a car crash, the mind might assign a meaning like, "It was an accident." It might tell you that it is not your fault. If the mind decides that this accident is not your fault, it likely assigns the feelings of anger, denial, and blame. Whereas if the mind decides, "I am responsible," it might go on to assign the feeling of guilt and fear of consequences.

Because the feelings and emotions of the body, mind, and soul are intimately connected, we have difficulty discerning one from the other. The mind and body are tangible, whereas the soul is rather intangible. The fact that we descend into the third dimension with amnesia about the truth of our duality compounds the confusion surrounding the separation of physical and nonphysical self.

When we ascend from unconsciousness of our duality into

consciousness of our duality, we achieve a state of *enlightenment*. This recognition is commensurate with an elevation of our frequency. In a broader context, the whole of humanity must undergo ascension at some point along their winding paths of existences. The conditions on our planet foretell that every individual being who is born on Earth must incur a physical death in order to leave the 3.0 dimension. In the moment of physical death, it is imperative for the energy body to separate from the physical body. On a very rudimentary level, the energy body must go somewhere. Each of us has a choice in the directionality of our soul's journey. Will you make a conscious choice to ascend or will you settle for the default condition?

Each being will transcend the body in some way at death—we have no choice. The direction of a dying person's ascension will depend on the vibration of the dying person's energy body at the time of the physical death. Some souls will ascend to a higher-vibrational dimension, some will remain in a third-dimensional state, and others will descend into the astral planes that exist at a lower frequency than our Earth's. Every soul desires to ascend and have the next embodied experience in a more enlightened, higher-frequency realm.

Multidimensional travel is not a required step of ascension but a privilege. Activating the dormant ability to travel consciously out of body before death is something that most incarnated beings won't experience. Fortunately, multidimensional travel is not the goal; it merely demonstrates what is possible for each divine being embodied on the planet.

The ability to "wake up," or accept the truth about your dual nature, is an inherent ability you possess in the very core of your being. However, to begin the process of ascension you must want enlightenment to the point of needing the truth to go on living.

This is to say, you must be relentless in your pursuit of knowing the truth about who you really are. This pursuit of knowing will awaken you to your innate powers. You may find that you have the power of conscious multidimensional travel within you. There are numerous energetic abilities that lie within our DNA framework. Your abilities are waiting for you to activate them through your conscious awakening.

In this life, we are programmed to look outside ourselves for answers. We require validation from others for acceptance. We tend not to trust ourselves because we do not know who we are and are taught early on to trust and learn from others' interpretations of the facts. But the answers are within us, as they have always been. Waking up to consciousness is an introspective pursuit.

In general, we are unaccustomed to looking inward for validation and truth. We tend to rarely trust ourselves or listen to our intuition. We look for outside evidence to determine if the power of the Universe we perceive is real. We sabotage our own power to manifest desires with low-frequency thoughts involving fear and doubt. We live in fear of past situations repeating themselves and are unsettled by the mystery of the future. Moreover, we tend to neglect the present moment of well-being in favor of giving credence to past disappointments or perceived failures. Your past experiences do not determine your future. It is only the power you give to your past that allows it to be relived again and again.

Let's take a moment and think about a past situation that perhaps you fear will show up again in the future, like a pattern or cycle repeating itself in life. Let's look closer at an undesirable money situation where there never seems to be enough money at the end of the month. Every month, there is a choice to be made about what bill gets paid and which ones will have to wait. In this state of mind, you may feel a sense of panic or fear. You might experience pain in your gut, lose your appetite, or experience your heart racing as your mind searches for immediate solutions. Perhaps you've seen this enough times that you now believe you can't tolerate the pain, so you medicate yourself with alcohol or other drugs, so you won't feel the torment in the moment that it is surfacing. Some will experience agony so severe related to money troubles that they'd sooner die than face the monetary shortfall.

Rest assured that painful, emotional cycles like this one can be successfully transmuted. Once it is transformed you will begin to experience situations related to money very differently and leave the past where it belongs.

So how do we transmute this situation? It starts with acknowledging it. You must see this as an emotional pattern being expressed from the soul level. The emotions you harbor related to a situation or circumstance take residence in your heart center and indeed have a claim on your being. When you begin to feel the familiar feelings related to unworthiness, lack, insecurity, embarrassment, shame, and fear, hear them by acknowledging their presence. You see, these feelings *want* to be addressed and transmuted; that is precisely why you are experiencing them. Your body does not want to continue processing these worrisome feelings either. Over time, such heavy feelings in the emotional body can and will bring harm to the physical body.

Acknowledging a persistent cycle of emotions can take the

form of simply saying to yourself "Okay, I hear you." Ask yourself where this feeling comes from. You may find that a childhood memory comes to mind or a past situation from another time in your life formulates from the far recesses of your memories. Find the time and place to be quiet and really address these feelings. As the memories and associated feelings rise within you, take several deep, focused breaths and allow the feelings to pass. It will not be comfortable at first but allow yourself to feel nonetheless. You will not be given more to process than you can handle. As you are consciously breathing, forgive yourself or others associated with the worrisome circumstance. Then ask yourself to transmute the troubling feelings into feelings of freedom and forward change. Ask yourself what you can do to let go of the pain forever. Confirm with your higher self that you are ready to release these hurtful feelings and move forward in life. Have every confidence in yourself that you are enough and stronger than any circumstance put before you.

As you move through this exercise, notice how your feelings begin to change. Notice the changes in your body. Depending on how deep the pain, you will likely repeat this exercise several times over as many months. What you will notice is that each time it gets a little easier and hurts a little less. As you move through time and space, you will notice new possibilities showing up for you in the area of your finances and every other aspect of life. You will be shown other areas of your past that also need to be released. Now equipped with the tools to transform and release dense energies, transmuting the rest of your troubled past will be a piece of cake. The act of releasing energies from your past heals you and holds within it the power to proactively change your future.

Although we came to Earth equipped to have fulfilling lives, we arrived with a level of amnesia about our true dual nature. Almost everybody currently alive was taught an unfulfilling way of life by members of past generations who were largely dense minded. Sure, there have always been a few enlightened individuals among us, people who figured things out, but these beings have been too few and too far between.

We have taken human form because there are lessons to learn, deliberate challenges to face, and missions to accomplish here on Earth. Not everyone chooses to wake up while embodied. It is only by going through a deep, introspective process that enlightenment is earned. It is from the personal desire to know thyself that the true self is revealed.

CHAPTER 4

The Ascension Process

Let's talk some more about ascension since it is the ultimate reason we were born. Ascension is the process of knowing your true self and becoming one with the Source energy. This is a forever-unfolding process that for every individual soul spans eons and multiple incarnations. Everything in existence is in perpetual forward motion, changing and evolving. Even Source energy itself is a learning body that has an ascension path. Although Source energy is the root of all life, it is an intelligent energy that learns from the multiplicity of incarnations that it ultimately will be unifying.

The initial stage of the human ascension process is knowing that you are more than just a physical body. That you are a complex being that exists in multiple dimensions. This is not a belief or something that you can have faith in. It is something that you must implicitly know about yourself. You must accept that your current earthly existence is only one of your many incarnations. If you are now waking up to your higher self, consider this a gift for bravely enduring a lengthy and circuitous past of learning and evolving.

That said, knowing that you are more than a physical body does not diminish the importance of this embodiment or the importance of any other you will have in the future.

Embodiment is a highly orchestrated system that enables souls to survive in a dense elemental world. Your body is a vastly sophisticated instrument that allows you to interpret the emotions and feelings of your energy body in a physical setting. The physical-energetic symbiosis typifies the duality of being. To truly know that you are more than a just a physical body requires the release of all previously accepted labels and false "truths" you have used to define yourself. At the end of acceptance of your duality, you are left with the indisputable insight: *I am divine energy having a human experience.* Everything else you have called yourself or believed about yourself is merely part of the illusion of the third dimension.

The next imposing step is to release all that you think you know so that you can be ready to accept what *is*. This ostentatious posture is arguably the most challenging. It takes the work of releasing every past and present understanding of your physical incarnations. You must release eons of pain, struggles, and emotional blockages. There is a great deal of un-learning that accompanies enlightenment.

You likely are holding on to some relics from your past that you are unaware of carrying. The work of ascension is not done alone. In the process of accepting your duality, you begin to know your higher self. On the journey of self-discovery, you also find that you have many guides who are ready and willing to assist you on your path of awakening. You must call out to them for help with this necessary step of releasing baggage of multiple previous incarnations.

One evening on my ascension path, I set the intention to meet my ethereal guides. I had heard a lot about them but had not yet experienced the visible presences of my guides. Certainly, I assumed I had some guardians working with me on some level because there had been many situations in my life where I felt that I had experienced divine intervention. In my early days of multidimensional travel, I never felt alone and occasionally I would hear voices speaking to me, so assumed I was being supported by guides or by my higher self, but I never observed anyone. I would only feel a palpable presence.

So, as I lay down to sleep that night, I asked my higher self to help me meet these infamous guides. I wanted to be introduced and see what they looked like. Soon I began traveling.

In my conscious dream, I found myself in a new apartment. As I looked around, it seemed rather empty. Apparently, I lived there alone and would come and go, engaging in the daily activities of life. Nothing appeared unusual about my situation. However, as I walked into the rather spacious bathroom, I saw a large group of beings quietly standing around. The number was in the dozens and they lined all the walls. These beings appeared ancient and of a forgotten culture. I was startled to see them standing there, so I quickly left the bathroom . . . only to find dozens more beings setting up sleeping cots in my living room.

I didn't feel any fear. I was just surprised to see all these people in my house. I finally asked, "What is everyone doing here and why are people hiding in my bathroom?"

Then I heard my higher self say, "You said you wanted to meet your guides."

I replied with a hefty "Oh" of understanding that woke me up into my physical reality.

Every living being, including you and me, has ethereal guides that have always been there during every incarnation. Many spirit guides go unacknowledged throughout an entire lifespan. We also have guides that are in physical bodies just as we are. These sentient beings show up as our teachers, mentors, friends, and family members. Whether you awaken to consciousness or not, you have access to many of your guides and guardians. Beings are looking out for you here on the planet as well as in the farthest reaches of the cosmos.

We are indeed never alone.

Releasing all that you think you know encompasses learned knowledge about the physical world, everything you believe about yourself, and every belief you have regarding your existence. The physical mind is limited in what it can comprehend and interpret. We can never know everything about the Earth or Multiverse from an intellectual perspective. You must resign to the awareness of what *is*.

Ascension requires letting go of antiquated belief systems that are limited to a third-dimensional existence. In this way, you will expand your awareness. This is not to suggest that what you have learned about the physical world is wrong, just that it is hopelessly incomplete. All human constructs and beliefs surrounding religion, money, time, and race will be challenged and debunked as you travel on the path of conscious awareness. (The human constructs will be discussed in later chapters.)

You will be tasked with seeing through all that humankind has created, so you may bear witness to everything in creation that remains unseen by the physical eye.

Early in the process of letting go, you are likely to begin releasing emotions that are fresh and on the surface. You will be shown experiences from your current life that need reconciliation and healing. You will likely have familial relationships in need of repair. You will have to clear your own baggage and forgive yourself in the same way that you forgave others. Forgiveness begins with acceptance of your role and the role of others in creating negative feelings or bad blood between yourself and another being.

Here's a process you might use to clear the air with another person. Find a way to reestablish communication. If this cannot be done safely, set a high intention that your thoughts and words of forgiveness reach the recipient. You might write a letter that you never send to express and work out your grievances. The point is to find a way, by yourself, to achieve closure in the most honest way possible.

When your intention to forgive is empowered with truth, genuine apologies and acknowledgments are heard even if a recipient is not in an energetic place to receive or respond to such messages, fully or in person. When forgiveness is granted and accepted in earnest, you find that there was really nothing at all to forgive. You see, we are all here on Earth to have self-evolutionary learning experiences. There are no mistakes, accidents, or coincidences.

Underlying most conflicts is a misunderstanding. All beings incarnated in the third dimension today have forgotten who they are and why they are here. As dense-minded human beings, we have become distracted from our purpose as souls and separated from our Source energy. Most of us routinely intoxicate ourselves with any number of vices, substances, or physical behaviors in an attempt to fill the void that is a byproduct of the amnesia about who we are. We carry so much heavy baggage throughout our lives that we are blind to our true selves.

Because we cannot recognize each other on a soul level, it's difficult to understand that we are all interconnected. But we are! We are all part of the same remarkable, everlasting Source. Much of the pain we feel in our hearts and minds is a direct result of being disconnected from our eternal essence.

The process of letting go is an energetic clearing process. For this to be successful, fully allow the feelings that emerge from within you during the clearing process to arise. Keep breathing and remain focused on your breath. By allowing and being present with the feelings and then transmuting them with the power of your breath, you begin to elevate your vibrational frequency.

You may have to repeat this process many times over several months, even years. It does not matter how long it takes, each attempt is helpful. Every transmuted emotion brings you closer to ascension. The more you practice the releasing process, the easier it becomes.

The idea is not to go through life emotionless. Allow yourself to feel and then to discharge negative emotions. Instead of acting in ways that are unbecoming of a divine being, when a strong negative emotion arises, use your breath—inhaling and exhaling fully and slowly—until the feeling passes. It is most helpful in these situations to remember who you are, reminding yourself of your power, strength, and abilities.

You may need to pace the room and have time alone to do this to completion. Grant yourself the time and space you need to go through the process.

Rid yourself of old patterns of screaming, striking, yelling, or verbally cursing anyone. Such behavior is not effective at releasing the energy of negative emotions and old karma. *Karma* is a term describing the phenomenon of cause and effect whereby actions in a previous time or existence have consequences in your future. Just as there is negative karma and consequences, there is also positive karma. The idea I am promoting here is *transmutation*.

Given that negative energy—like all energy—cannot be created or destroyed, it must be transmuted. The letting go process is the transmuting of dense or negative energy into lighter, higher-frequency energy. This does not have to be a grand transmutation, as from hate to love; it can be a smaller shift, like the transmutation to inner peace and acceptance.

There are a great many things in the world to feel angry about or disgusted by. What is important to remember in these instances is that everybody on Earth is learning and each of us descends to the planet rather confused. This is not an excuse for corrupt behavior but rather a chance to feel compassion. I know when I see or hear of something that hurts me to the depth of my soul, I pain for the torment that embodied being must be experiencing. This can be even more challenging when something horrible happens to you. But know that in every situation imaginable there is room for learning and forgiveness. Sometimes the forgiveness is for yourself.

Breathing through the pains of the past primes your heart chakra to again open. The heart center is both the fourth chakra down from the crown and up from the root chakra which lies at the base of the spine—a midpoint in the torso where the lower self and the higher self are brought into harmony. Its vibrational resonance is represented by the color green.

When your heart center opens, you will feel compassion flooding your energy body. The sensation of this in your physical body will be remarkable—like love energy spreading from your physical heart and radiating through your entire body, which is tingling and coming to life with a new vibrancy. Only when the anger, fear, and pain are replaced by love and compassion will you know that you have entirely transmuted an emotion and its karma.

You must find a way to forgive and love yourself the same as everybody else. You are not alone, as everyone must transform lifetimes of pain into love to ascend into a frequency of conscious awareness. Have unyielding compassion for yourself as a practice because now you know that you have endured eons of emotional trials on your chosen path.

Letting go of all religious beliefs and aligning with the truth of how the Universe operates—let's call it the *universal edict*—presents its own unique challenges. While elevating your frequency, there will be opportunities to experience life in different dimensions. The religious institutions of the third dimension are not supported beyond Earth 3.0. There is faith, of course, but not in an institution, another person, a statue, or a book. Faith is grounded within you and your eternal connection to the Source energy.

How the Multiverse is ordered and organized is not up for interpretation by the physical mind. It represents all that is, and, as human beings, we cannot comprehend all that is. What is visible to us, and thus what we believe, is extremely narrow in its perspective.

Conscious awareness does not ask you to believe, it beckons you to know. Consciousness is not an intellectual pursuit. It is a manner of being. All the information about your dual nature and all that *is*, is already within you. It is encoded in your physical DNA. You are tasked with becoming aware of the internal knowing and with trusting yourself. Each of us—there are no exceptions—is highly intuitive. But our dense nature as physical entities foster separation of our true selves, while inside of embodiments, from the Source. This separation has created a pervasive ignorance of the true self and of the ultimate truth surrounding our existence.

Because we lack knowledge of the truth about ourselves we do not know other fundamental truths about the totality of existence. Furthermore, there have been deliberate actions by beings holding positions of power to hide the inner knowledge from us that has always been within us. Efforts to suppress the omnipotent power of the individual in favor of authoritative power of a designated few, have a long and inglorious place in our human history. Some religions that held divine frequencies in past ages no longer hold the vibrational frequencies consistent with ascension today. Holding tightly to any religious beliefs will impede the ascension process for anyone not willing to release them.

All beliefs carry thoughts and feelings with them, thus holding onto a part of your divine (Source) energy. To ascend the third dimension, you must reclaim the energy held hostage to archaic belief systems. Your energy body in its entirety is required for you to complete the ascension process. Completion and restoration of the whole must be accomplished if you are to declare mastery and a rightful place on the ascensions path. The vibrational frequency required to ascend the third dimension cannot be achieved if the emotional pain from past relationships, limiting belief systems, or other aspects of your physical life are retained.

Ascension is a wholly encompassing experience. Each being on the path of ascension will be charged with completing tasks associated with clearing dense energy along the way. Only when all limiting belief systems are transformed to the satisfaction of the ascended masters—a group of ethereal beings that govern our soul development on Earth—will crossing into a higher dimension be allowed. Even the most enlightened beings in human form today have clearing exercises to accomplish to gain this privilege. The limitations of the human mind prevent us from having a full appreciation of the legions of past emotions in need of release.

CHAPTER 5

Elevating Your Frequency

The body must be attuned to tolerate higher-vibrational frequencies. Radio frequency can help explain energetic frequency. Think of an old-fashioned radio with a hand-operated dial and various frequencies marked on the display. As the dial is turned, it tunes into these different frequencies or *airwaves,* as they used to be known. The radio signals are always broadcasting but you cannot hear programs or music playing on the station unless you dial into the correct frequency. Like a radio dial, your life energy must be attuned to a higher vibration to raise your frequency. Tuning the energy body, however, is not as easy or simple as turning a radio dial. It requires the process of introspection and interpersonal growth to elevate personal frequency.

What must change in you to elevate your frequency? To begin, you must change your thought processes and emotional responses to common life situations.

Imagine you suddenly lose your job and become fearful that you cannot make ends meet. It is perfectly rational to be concerned. The mind creates this discomfort because there is a physicality to living on Earth that requires us to have access to resources, such as the physical thing called *money.* We have collectively created an environment on Earth where almost everything we need to survive must be purchased. The modern lifestyle has its costs. However, in the same way we tend to forget that our true self is not physical, we tend to forget that everything in the world, at its very core, including money, is also made of pure energy and connected to Source, like us.

The feeling of abundance resonates at a higher frequency than scarcity. A fearful emotion that comes from a place of conceptualizing lack will attract experiences that resonate with the dense energy of scarcity of resources. The higher emotion of happiness or fulfillment that comes from a place of visualizing abundance attracts the higher frequency outcomes associated with an increase of resources.

The common thread that runs through the fear of joblessness and scarcity in this example is uncertainty about the future. If you can be with the uncertainty, acknowledging the fear and allowing it to pass through you, you can elevate the frequency of your energy body. This type of fearlessness comes from trusting in the broader Universe, which holds infinite possibilities.

It is good practice to trust that there is a natural order to things and that many possibilities are unknown. Because all possibilities are not in your awareness does not mean they unavailable to you. There are things we know: the *knowns*. Things we know that we do not know: the *known unknowns*. And things we do not know that we do not know: the *unknown unknowns*. These unknown unknowns are the things that you do not know exist for you which are still possibilities at higher frequency. Trust in these as you clear your negativity.

On Earth we live in a time construct as well as a money construct. When a job loss occurs, the issue of time complicates the picture because elevating your vibrational frequency regarding money also takes *time*. This is one of the hardest parts of moving through the time construct. Though you may be making incremental steps, trusting in the universal order of things and elevating your frequency, the changes in your job and money situation do not change overnight. Use the time it takes to do your work of introspection and continue steadfast on your ascension path as the outer world catches up with your inner state. In the process, you will find your reality changing in certain, sometimes surprising ways. The process will necessitate your resourcefulness, testing your patience. It will also strengthen your resolve.

It has been said that all in life is a test. Who you are in the face of the challenge determines to a large degree your vibrational frequency. True security comes from being secure in moments of greatest uncertainty. All other security is false. Relationships change, jobs are lost and found, and things come and go. Permanence does not truly exist in life. Everything is in a constant state of flux. The ebb and flow must be embraced as it is required for forward movement. Joblessness is the test. Divorce is the test. Sickness is the test. And so on.

Begin to see the daily obstacles that confront you as the tools they are for elevating your frequency. Allow all the changes in your life to be evolutionary.

In the beginning of the ascension process, it is easy to feel foolish believing in the ultimate power of the Multiverse. Intending to be in alignment with this energy is not exactly sanctioned thinking or conventional wisdom. It takes a lot of courage to tell yourself "It's going to be okay" and truly believe it in the face of uncertainty.

At a very young age we are taught to distrust our inner selves and to search for physical facts to validate our feelings. It is this kind of stifling of the true self that contributes to our forgetfulness. To begin to remember again is to dismantle centuries of consensus beliefs that have moved us away from looking inward in favor of looking outward.

There are many aspects of life that must be addressed in the process of developing conscious awareness of the duality of your being and all this makes possible. The first question to ask yourself is "Who am I?" The first action to take is that of forgiveness.

I was born in February 1972, four months ahead of my mother's eighteenth birthday, her second child. With no more than a tenth-grade education, my mother attempted to raise me and my older brother along with the three other children she would soon have. Four of us survived to adulthood. One of us did not. In my youth, I could not comprehend that my mother was not more than a mere child herself. Like all children, I expected the very most of her despite every limiting circumstance.

My childhood was not a bright, colorful one. It was not rich in resources or culture. I do not have memories of Mom and Dad and happy family scenes when I recall my childhood. Life appeared daunting and shamefully hard. There was no higher value given to education in our household, no imperative issued to better myself. "Getting out" was a journey that we children had to forge on our own if we dared try. There was not even a hint of the promise of security. There were few upward expectations, and everyone appeared to be existing in a state of perpetual strife and melancholy. The bar was cripplingly low for me: at finishing high school and not getting pregnant while still a teen.

Of course, there were occasional happy memories scattered

about, especially from events early on, but my childhood is not one that I would wish to repeat.

There is absolutely no one to blame for the lack and blitheness I experienced. These are simply my perceptions of my childhood.

Before I was old enough to remember having an intact family, my parents divorced. After that, my siblings and I and a few cousins of mine were raised by my paternal grandmother, a woman who was in the throes of raising nine children of her own. We were very poor, living in an inadequate housing project in a rundown town. We survived on very little with the help of government rations. I rarely saw my mother after the bitter divorce. Therefore, my father was the prominent parental figure of visible memory in my formative life.

When I was six years old, my father remarried, and our family moved from Brownsville, Pennsylvania, to Morgantown, West Virginia. By the time I reached ten years of age, my birth mother had moved far away from me, across the country to Colorado. I didn't realize that it would be nineteen years before I would see or speak to her again.

Between age ten and twenty-nine, I felt abandoned by my mother. I judged her for not being in my life and secretly blamed her for the emptiness that had taken residence inside me. I was detached from my feelings, from people, from things. I was on a treadmill of earning successes to validate my worth. I wanted my mother to feel sorry for not wanting me or being a part of my life and to harbor a shame so deep it would pain her very existence. I aspired to greatness just to show her that I was good enough, hoping she would regret that she had abandoned me. Despite generating these successes, I was left unfulfilled with an overwhelming void that could not be filled no matter the achievement.

Before I could see what was really happening, I had graduated college, lived abroad in West Africa for a year, worked as a pharmaceutical chemist, and was completing my final year of medical school.

One afternoon in my final year of medical school, I received a call telling me that my mother was in a coma. The news affected me in ways unexpected. It was then that I realized how deep my feelings were for the woman who had brought me into this life. Despite our years of separation, I felt an innate connection to her and rushed to her ICU bedside several states away. When I arrived, I recognized her straight away despite the many years that had passed and her intubated condition.

I sat with my mother until she was well enough to awaken and breathe on her own. It was then that I realized that the time that had passed had taken a toll on all of us; on me, on my brothers, and on our mother. We had all suffered in some measurable, visceral way. From the doctors, I learned that my mother had overdosed on antidepressants. It turned out that she too carried a deep sadness and a crevasse void inside her.

Upon her recovery, my mother and I finally had time to talk. My mother had never seen me as an adult so there was much for us to learn about one another. It would take several years, but we began to heal our relationship by simply talking to one another again. On one occasion, my mother came to visit me in while I was living in Southern California. We attended an awareness conference together and toured around Los Angeles and Santa Barbara. It was at that time that I told my mother I loved her and that I finally understood how young she had been when I was born. Then I forgave her. I forgave her for not being there because I knew she felt incapable.

My mother told me that she hadn't meant to leave me. That she was unable to care for me or my brothers. And as more time passed, it was harder and harder for her to make the call to reconnect with us. Upon uttering the words, *I forgive you,* I felt a complete and total cathartic release. Then I also forgave myself for the years of judgment and blame I had put on her. We spilled many tears together in the enlightened state of forgiveness.

After that, I was no longer holding onto any of the heaviness I had previously felt when it came to my mother. I didn't have the pain anymore. I no longer wept inside upon hearing her name. I was finally free.

As children, we do not have the perspective of seeing our parents as infants, at a time when they were new and unburdened. But imagine if only for an instant you did get to see your parents as babies without any of the encumbrances they have carried throughout their lives. Imagine your parents with no mistakes or worries. No stress. No political or religious views. No vices, judgments, or habits. Completely devoid of any irritating manners of being. In that precise moment of perceiving their true selves, you would be overwhelmed with unconditional love for them. You would witness them still connected to Source energy. Fully supported. Free of pain and worry. You would become overwhelmed with the emotion of genuine love.

This is how your parents once saw you. Only the physical eye sees the outer shell of a being and make some type of judgment. The physical eye is biased and subjective. How it interprets what it sees—as bad or good—to a large extent depends on past experiences. The mind does not behold the truth of a being's true divinity and purity as a spirit in the same way that the heart does. It can only perceive that which is occupying its direct vision and label it according to the imagination, which is filtered through beliefs.

It would be almost another decade before I became a mother myself and was able to fully understand how incredibly difficult it is to be a mother, even in the best of circumstances.

My birth mom died nine months after I gave birth to my son. She was fifty-six. I was able to bury her with a sense of peace about me. I trust that on some level she achieved a semblance of peace too. Nothing of importance was left unsaid between us. Though I wished I could have done more for her while she was alive, the most important thing I could have done was complete. Forgiveness was the most meaningful and sincere act I carried out during my mother's life. It allowed the both of us to make closure.

I have thought for a long time now that we weep at funerals because we have not made closure in life. It is one thing to miss the departed, it is another to have things left unsaid. It is vitally important to communicate with loved ones before they transcend their earthly life. We cannot know if we will ever meet again in another dimension. Where we land on the "other side" of life depends on the frequency of our energy at the time of death, not on the nature of the relationships we had on Earth.

Forgiveness was the first decisive step on my path to higher awareness.

I remember how light and free I felt at the time I forgave my mother and myself. I believed that if I could forgive her and heal our relationship then I could forgive anyone. It turns out that forgiveness is hard to give, particularly when a crime has been committed against you or a loved one or when hurt runs long and deep. This is true whether you are forgiving others or yourself.

Many people have had the experience of an absent parent. Though the absence may take many forms, know that just like you, your parents are on their own evolutionary paths. Every person who has a child is not necessarily equipped to care for a new life. It is not any person's place to judge the path of another.

Sometimes the pain someone inflicts is a direct reflection of their own inner struggle. In my case, the absence of my birth mother prepared me with the strength I needed to accomplish my purpose in life. It was imperative that I learn the art of forgiveness, so I could one day be free of emotional pain. That freedom has helped me become capable of soul flight. The ability to accept and let go is an early requirement on the path to expand your consciousness.

Heavy emotional energy must be felt in the body and transmuted into pure love energy through the heart center. This is a task many people refuse to take on. There is the expectation of immense suffering as intensely negative energy from the distant past is again felt. But in truth, your heart will not break. Within in it is an infinite capacity to love. The heart center is not limited and already knows all that has occurred within the soul. The love energy of the heart center knows what it is doing. You are safe to listen to this essence within you and move bravely into ascension.

Transforming energy can be as easy as allowing a feeling to arise while breathing deliberately in and out of your body and synchronizing your thoughts with your pulse.

As you experience a dense energy emerging, such as fear or anger, question the emotion. Ask yourself why the memory triggering this feeling bothers you so much. And note that the triggering event can be a memory from an hour earlier, the day before, or an incident forty years ago. If it isn't happening right now, it is a memory.

Then, in the moment, connect with a prominent pulse point in your body. Close your eyes, breathe, and feel your pulse. Keep breathing until the pain or fear dissipates and you emerge with a sense of calm.

As you begin to feel better and lighter, know that you have transmuted the emotion, and in doing so, elevated your vibrational frequency.

What is left after all limiting beliefs and triggered emotions are transformed is pure love. You will have come full circle and begun to remember exactly who you are when you reach this milestone. Trust that knowing your true self will be absolutely astounding.

To wake up to the true self requires a close examination of the self. Taking an inward look at yourself sometimes provokes the harshest criticism of any. You will not forgive everyone all at once or be able to instantly forgive yourself for all past transgressions. The path of enlightenment takes many lifetimes.

Some embark upon the path of forgiveness and ascension early in life and some never do at all. It is important to understand that it has taken many incarnations to awaken. Waking up in your current life implies a full circle of evolution from past eons. Even so, an accelerated awakening can take the sum of an entire lifespan.

Throughout your ascension, people, events, memories, and

physical things will show up to challenge your ability to forgive and see rightly. As you learn to acknowledge the feelings of past pains and allow them to pass through you, the act of forgiveness becomes easier and easier. The heaviness you feel at times will be lifted. And there will come a time when there is no resistance at all to what *is*. When a painful thought or feeling comes to you, you will simply accept it and move on, like inserting a ticket to go through a metro turnstile. As the energy body becomes wise, fear and anger will cause only mild ill feelings and in time, elicit no pain at all.

It is at this point that we come to realize that life just *is*. Life is not good or bad. It is our interpretation of events and cultural conditioning that assigns meaning to actions.

Elevation of your energetic frequency is both a physical and nonphysical journey. The ascension process strips the ego to nothingness. The ego is the "I" or "me" that we come to identify ourselves. For example: I am Catholic, male, female, a carpenter, an engineer, a wife, a husband, and so on. The ego has a place only in the physical realm. It is an adaptation to the third-dimensional environment of Earth 3.0 that helps us manage our physical existence.

The ego can become confused when the labels of the physical being are incongruent with the energy body. We often see this, for example, with contested gender assignments.

Where the ego is useful is in explaining our relation to things and people as well as our likes and dislikes. The ego belongs in a physical place and is not retained at higher frequencies. The energy body is not limited by the labels of humankind. It does not conform to any single physical existence or culture.

During your awakening and ascension, the ego must be

acknowledged for what it is, honored for its purpose, and ultimately its responses and thought patterns released. Attaching too tightly to the ego prevents flight.

The ego is a density not unlike fear or hate. Holding on to any of these energies will prevent movement into higher realms of consciousness.

Once the ego is fully released, you can begin to answer the question of "Who am I?" The first step in answering this question is to recognize that all human beings, like all life on Earth, are pure energy. Energy cannot be created or destroyed by us.

The ego is a manifestation of the human mind designed exclusively for survival in an earthly existence. Just as there is a separation between the physical self and the nonphysical self, there is also a separation between the ego and the true self.

Once there is an acceptance of the separation of ego and soul, you can begin to detach from both your physical body and your ego. This detachment will begin to foster a release from all beliefs, religions, time, and all previously defined labels. With time and active releasing of your attachments, you no longer need the old definitions to feel significant or whole. You will begin to know your importance at your very core. You will no longer have to try to believe your true nature, you will begin to *KNOW*.

The body and various other forms life takes on Earth are simply physicalities. One could argue that the forms we take are illusions. Essentially, we are all wearing costumes and playing different roles in various scenarios. The body or shell we each inhabit is indeed brilliant. It is designed to allow the energy body to interact within Earth's atmosphere and at a dense, material frequency. If we were here only as our true selves, imagine how many of the potential Earth experiences we are having that would be missed. The body is special despite the illusion. Therefore, it is important to care for and love the body.

Our bodies house and support our life energy. When traveling while still embodied, the physical body cannot make the journey. The distances we travel are far and the frequencies too high for it to tolerate. The body must be left behind. Like at death, the body stays while the soul departs.

To experience multidimensional travel while living, you must prepare the body by acclimating it to new frequencies. Acclimation is not something you can actively do. It is done by your higher self and your guides. The human body is unique and has tremendous value in the cosmos. All beings of higher energy take great care not to harm it. You should take great care of it as well. The body has within it the ability to attune the physical for experiences in higher-frequency dimensions. This latent ability may be activated by thoughts and actions geared toward emotional refinement.

When I travel out, I place my body in a safe, comfortable place. I will not travel out while driving a car or cooking over a hot stove, for example. These days I only travel when I am comfortable and safe in my bed.

It is imperative that all the body's immediate needs be met. The body must be healthy and fed. The body must be free of pain or irritation and the bladder must be empty. To travel out of body requires external efforts aimed at comfort and support while internal efforts are aimed at elevating your frequency.

Multidimensional travel requires that the body not be contaminated or intoxicated. In the past, many cultures used hallucinogenic plants to explore higher dimensions. Today, naturally available plants that were used in ancient times by indigenous people no longer hold the requisite frequency and potency to facilitate the same types of experiences. What tends to happen now is the mind-altering substances instigate negative experiences for the users—aka "bad trips." If any soul travel occurs at all, it may be to astral planes that have a lower frequency than Earth and thereby cannot generate enlightening experiences.

On one occasion, I was being tested. The limits of my frequency were being exercised to determine how much further I could travel out while still embodied. I arrived not at a place but at a frequency where I was met by one of my ethereal guides. At this point in my travels, I did not require earthlike imagery to feel comfortable anymore. I could travel very quickly, I thought, in complete darkness through the depths of the cosmos dotted with distant stars. Despite this, my guide decided to appear to me in what I would describe as a human hologram.

When I travel, I can always feel energy beings around me and communicate telepathically. When my guide took shape as a human, I was somewhat shocked and stated, "Why are you appearing to me this way?" I had so many questions I wanted to ask of much more value. Why I asked this low-priority question, I do not know. Nonetheless, in that moment, my guide disappeared and worked with me as pure energy.

During the exercise, my guide communicated with other beings in a type of technical language that I could not understand. What I did understand was the assessment itself. When I am being taken out, so to speak, it feels like someone is holding my hands or even holding me up. In this trial, I was being guided by hand. My guide held on to me and off we went, soaring through the cosmos at a pace beyond the speed of light.

The journey was difficult. It was a bumpy ride for me as it always is when I increase my frequency. I even thought I might detach, as the force was exceedingly strong. Nonetheless, I was able to complete the test before I returned to the base frequency at which I had begun.

I was waiting, as my guide was discussing yet another test he wanted to do with me, when the part of my energy body associated with my right foot began to ache. I thought, *Oh no, something is wrong with my body,* and wondered if I would have to immediately return and remedy it. I looked at my guide who was aware of my concern. Although I did not want to go back right away, I knew the priority the physical body has. My guide took me out for one final test and afterward I was not returned to base frequency, but to my body to address my foot.

Be forewarned that the first exposure to a higher frequency is rarely smooth. When embodied, there is a great amount of heat generated when the energy body travels. This can result in profuse sweating, particularly when traveling at the highest frequencies.

The body can also hear higher frequencies. As the body attunes, so do the ears. Hearing aspects of attunement takes a couple of forms. The first thing I noticed was hearing varied frequencies in my ears constantly. I found I could hear shifts in frequency that were aligned with the energy of the Multiverse. The cosmos is neither a quiet place nor a cold place. It is the human body that perceives cold, not the soul. On Earth, our ears are designed with bones and membranes to hear a range of frequencies necessary for our everyday existence. The energy body is attuned to something very different.

I recall that prior to traveling out of body I would routinely hear static when it was quiet around me. I didn't recall hearing anything in particular, just a subtle buzzing. Now I hear tones—not ringing or irritating sounds, but variable tones. Sometimes they are loud, other times the tones hum gently in the background. The constant is that the tones are always there.

The second change in hearing involves the true self. There are at least two voices in our heads. The mind or ego is speaking, and the higher self is speaking. Most of us cannot get past the mind's voice to ever hear the higher self even though the higher self has a more confident and powerful voice. When the higher self speaks, it does not dwell in the past but only in the present moment.

Unlike the ego's voice, the higher self's voice does not gossip or have a chip on its shoulder. It does not talk about events or ideas and does not fear or doubt. The higher self has a resolute voice that speaks the truth. But it takes quieting the ego to hear it. Quieting the mind requires practice as the scores of distractions and noise in daily life can easily override the voice of the higher self.

The human species has also lost the ability to truly listen because the ego voice is continuously chattering. When someone is talking to us, we have a nagging tendency to interrupt. When we are thinking about what we want to say, the listening quality diminishes. It is the egoic mind that is impatient, always having something to say. You must practice the lost art of listening if you wish to hear the voice of your higher self.

What does it sound like? Some describe it as hearing the voice of God in times of desperation or during an epiphany. That voice is you, the higher YOU, finally being heard. The higher self is in direct connection with the Source energy that some people refer to as God. The Source energy is not defined by gender or any other human trait. The Source is the omnipotent creator that conceives of all life in the Multiverse. Human beings are not superior to any other life forms in existence. Thereby, we do not lend our dense, limited prototype to the Source. The Source energy *is*. It always has been. It always will be.

CHAPTER 6

Being Quiet

Quieting the mind takes dedicated practice. In life today, we are bombarded with an endless stream of noises from television, news radio, music, internet videos, people talking, and video games, or simply the nagging voices inside our heads. The preponderance of ambient noise makes it almost impossible to grab a quiet moment in which we may simply be.

In other words, to be quiet requires effort.

The most onerous voice to silence is that of the ego, which is the voice of the mortal mind. Most of us are familiar with using techniques like deep breathing, mantra meditation, or a yoga practice to become mentally quiet. Apart from deep breathing, most practices like these are more effective when you establish a dedicated time or place to perform them.

A quiet mind is not static. Even if you achieve the state of having no thoughts, this state will be fleeting at best. That's the nature of the human mind: Thoughts will come and go and come and go again.

Life continues to happen regardless of how elevated our frequencies become. It is only through sustained practice that the ability to quiet the mind becomes a reliable occurrence and second nature to achieve. Even as ascension progresses, there must be continuous monitoring of thoughts. Not a cruel kind of monitoring like the police in East Germany during the Cold War, but the gentle monitoring like that of a mother with her new baby whom she has tender feelings for and wants to keep safe.

Your mind is necessary for your physical life and your thoughts won't just go away forever, permanently. Your mind will be with you throughout your current incarnation. However, it would be beneficial to the cause of ascension to tame it. I have often wondered if we are given our bodies not only to maintain but to mold them into our utmost beingness. Whether we are refining our appetite or our thoughts, it is a continues process requiring attention and diligence.

I learned to quiet the voice of my ego using all the previously stated techniques at one point or another. I started with mantra meditations that were as easy as stating "One, two" or "In, out" in coordination with my breathing. The idea was to pare down my thoughts to two simple words. I also engaged in a yoga practice that included several different deep-breathing techniques. My favorite style of yoga is intuitive yoga where the movements are slow enough to coordinate each movement with the breath.

I have always found maintaining a dedicated meditation practice challenging. Finding the time and space for it always seemed impossible considering the givens of my daily life. That said, under the right circumstances I have enjoyed participating in guided meditations. Despite earnest efforts, for a long time I found focus to be elusive.

The most effective way to quiet my mind came to me after my separation from my son's father. In January 2015, I moved out of our family home and into my own apartment. It wasn't the nicest place, but it was the least disruptive location I could afford. It was close by my son's school, adequate, safe, and warm. For one full year, I did not furnish the apartment beyond the very basics. I prepared only my son's room comfortably. I had a small sofa, two chairs, and one television that sat on the floor. In my own bedroom, I had only a mattress that lay on the floor. I had no light, no lamps, no nightstand. Nothing.

During the same one-year period, when I drove myself to work, I would not turn on the radio. Beyond the hum of road noise, this gave me at least thirty minutes of quiet each morning and evening. I limited my human contact outside of doing business. I rarely spoke on the telephone or socialized with friends, and I did not date. Despite the three years of spontaneous out-of-body travel I had already experienced, that was the year I became most attuned with my true self. It was the year I learned to be quiet.

During my first few attempts to quiet myself, past grievances would flood my mind. I would feel myself getting angry as I relived past pains and hurt feelings. It was during those moments, whether I was rushing to ready myself in the morning or driving on the road, that I would speak firmly and directly to myself, saying silently, *Susan, enough! It's over.* I would not allow myself to dwell on the past. I breathed deeply in and out until the wounded and resentful thoughts passed. I would still feel the pain and frustration of the situation I was recalling, but instead of acting on this information in any way that might distract me from the thoughts or feelings, I would just breathe.

If you think you recognize this as the technique I shared in Chapter 5, "Elevating Your Frequency," you are right. It is the same. Not only does this technique raise your vibration, it is mentally quieting to fully accept and embrace whatever is within you.

In the beginning, I would have to repeat this breathing process several times a day. My mind was so full of nonsense, it took me months to clear it of the residue of past experiences. I repeated the breathing and self-talk so frequently that it became second nature to me. As soon as a foul thought would enter my head, I would hear myself breathing. Over time, the pain became less and less, and I could stop a thought before it was completely formalized. Once I mastered this technique, I realized that I had found peace; a transient peace of mind. In this place of quiet, my tolerance for bothersome outside noise also diminished.

I could no longer listen to or read inflammatory news. I could not listen to gossip or the conversation of dense-minded people. It became too painful to hear petty gibberish in any of its numerous forms. Of course, intolerance of noise does not mean that noise is gone. In my case, I simply do not tune in to it. If I do hear the news, it is my processing of and reaction to it that has changed. The world remains a complex place with endless disturbances. I still feel empathy, sadness, or pain when seeing or hearing of distressing situations. The pain, however, is no longer as deep and does not fuel anger within me. No longer holding pent-up anger goes a long way in quieting the mind.

I have learned that our reactions to common painful situations can mature. Although none of us is the same person throughout life, we may display the same reaction to similar situations throughout our lives. We can, however deliberately modify our responses by changing the significance we attach to an emotionally triggering experience. Mature reactions and alternate reactions are rarely modeled for children by the adults in their lives, so we must take responsibility for learning them on our own—take responsibility for our own personal growth. There is always a choice in how we react to any situation even if that choice is to have no reaction at all.

Take the experience of failure. When a child fails at something, he will likely become frustrated and cry. He may even throw things, yell at others, or insult himself. This same reaction and behavior toward failure is also seen among many adults.

An alternate way of seeing failure is that it is a step in the direction of change, moving us toward success. Failure is an exercise in trial and error and an opportunity for growth.

If you are emotionally triggered by failure, instead of beating yourself up or destroying things when there is an adverse outcome, breathe and take some time to clear your mind. Write a log of what you've learned. What would you do differently next time? What wouldn't you do again? Congratulate yourself for taking the first steps toward change and growth. Forgive yourself for your perceived mistakes. Forgive others who do not recognize you or your inner process. Failures are instruments of learning and very necessary. No person is born on Earth knowing how to do anything at all. Anyone who has achieved great success has incurred many failures along the way. As painful as it might be perceived, this is how we learn.

Use this process to mature your responses to other types of painful experience and you'll soon find yourself becoming less reactive. Multidimensional travel has taught me not to assign judgment to events or situations. I am now an observer who feels emotions but does not assign meaning. The difference now is that I can almost immediately release the dense emotions of sadness, anger, and frustration. These low-energy emotions no longer control my thoughts or actions. The ability to feel and release is a supreme state of being, allowing one freedom from the mind.

Inner quietude is a manner of being. It is not an affirmation or meditation exercise. Because the mind is so loud and dominant when there is lack of awareness, you must first practice being quiet in an effort to release the ego's hold on your mind. Once your ego begins to dissolve, inner quiet will begin to replace your mind's chatter by effortlessly releasing that which comes to it but is not serving your higher self. As the mind chatter lessens and softens, the distinction between your ego and your true self will become more evident. You must want this clarity as your mind will not readily release its grip. After all, the mind desires routine and comfort. Any change at all is sure to disrupt the status quo as far as the mind is concerned.

Distinguishing between the mind's voice and the voice of the higher (true) self can be difficult at first. Part of the challenge is learning to recognize the true self. Knowing the true self is a deep personal desire on the path of expanding consciousness. Most people are content to remain ignorant of their duality of being. This perpetual state of detachment of the higher and lower self creates an energetic dissonance within the soul.

To know the true self is to accept that there are no defining labels of gender, occupation, or beliefs encumbering the soul. The true self is an energetic frequency vibrating within the physical body. The true self can vibrate at very low frequencies when the physical being is caught up in falsehoods, hate, jealousy, doubt, or fear. It will be vibrating at a low frequency during times of self-shaming, anger, or other forms of emotional pain.

It will be vibrating at a high frequency during times of love, joy, gratitude, confidence, and compassion. The ability to hear the voice of the true self requires a quieting of the mind.

The context of the messages you receive from your true self will be in reference to your needs or true purpose. An immature mind is loud—obnoxiously so. It is so loud, in fact, that it can easily override the voice of the true self. The unaware person becomes easily confused about what the ego-mind wants versus what the true self needs, so let's look at them individually, beginning with the ego-mind.

The mind (aka ego-mind) will always work to secure the physical body because that is its purpose. It wants security because it cannot know the future with any certainty. The mind will work to set up the future in a manner that is predictable. The mind is, however, limited to the confines of its perceived possibilities, or in other words, what it thinks is possible. It rarely imagines infinite possibilities because it relies on probabilities based on past learning or experience. The mind, therefore, positions the body in such a way to receive what is most probable in a given situation and prepares itself likewise.

When the mind realizes that the future is not what it imagined, it becomes uncomfortable and at times paralyzed. Some minds are so conditioned that even a pleasant surprise will be unwelcomed as people become shaken in disbelief or go into shock. It is the mind's rigorous conformity to a routine that prevents people from dreaming big or wanting more. As such, less probable options simply fall out of an individual's realm of possibilities.

The true self does not doubt or worry. Worrying is a choice made by the mind to trick the mind into thinking it is doing something useful in a certain situation. The mind believes there is always something to be done, even if it is worrying. This variety of mind chatter is essentially a clipping of wings that prevents flight. Instead of forward shifting, which is how the true self thinks, if your mind is dominating your thoughts, there is a redundant circular motion. In this state of being, memories of past or present concerns go around and round in your head. The mind moves in these circles because it desires comfort and familiarity, even if what is familiar is painful. Moments of frequency elevating change are rife with uncertainties that rattle the mind. The mind is never concerned with elevating your frequency — it is not what the mind is designed to do.

The true self has needs and purpose beyond the physical world; it requires the wheels of change to be in motion to elevate your frequency. It therefore asks you to move forward in the face of fear and ambiguity. And this is where growth occurs.

When it comes to personal growth and the matter of raising your vibration, it is not rational or useful to compare yourself to others. The most meaningful comparison is between your past self and present self. Are you happier now than you were in the past? More aware? More awake? Wiser? What steps could you begin to take to become the future self you desire to be?

Consciousness does not originate in the mind. It is rooted in the intangibles of emotions, in the sensations we call feelings. Study of the mind will help to explain wakefulness to this reality. Consciousness, however, is to be felt and to become aware of. It can only be understood from the perspective of journeying inward, into yourself. Although the mind may ultimately process what it means to be conscious, the mind or brain's transmission of signals is not the place of origination or domicile of consciousness. Consciousness lies in the metaphysical realm and exists both in concert with and in the absence of the body.

Humankind collectively has yet to understand what consciousness truly is. Most of us are too preoccupied with external stimuli to recognize consciousness. Scientifically, it is onerous to use the physical instruments we possess at our current state of technology to quantify and define consciousness. Fortunately, each of us can experience consciousness on our own. It is not, ultimately, a thing to be measured. It is the very essence of being.

CHAPTER 7

Sleep and Rest

Paying attention to the amount and quality of the sleep you are getting will go a long way in elevating your frequency. Sleep is the ideal body condition in which to revitalize the soul. Getting quality sleep each night is essential for the ascension process. For the benefit of your physical body and emotions, you require sleep that is not interrupted by the distractions of a television, a smartphone, or a beeper. Get in the habit of putting your smartphone in airplane mode overnight and establish a Do Not Disturb schedule for your designated sleeping hours.

There are occasions in life where low-quality sleep is temporarily expected. Sleeplessness over newborn babies will not disrupt your ascension path. Babies are reminders of our capacity to experience unconditional love. In this way, they are uniquely special.

Babies require a considerable amount of sleep, more than adults, in part because of their accelerated growth rate in infancy as well as their continued conscious connection to Source energy. This connection gives newborns the quality of pureness to which we are all unconsciously attracted. The soul will travel in and out of the body to help the newly incarnated being acclimate to its physical life form. It takes persistence for a life energy to become accustomed to being confined to a small, dense physical body.

Because of the difficulty of this transition, it is necessary for the sleep of infants to be hygienic and free of unhealthy distractions. The sound of a mother's heartbeat can be helpful in soothing the baby because it closely resonates with the frequency signature of the Universe. The infant will be genuinely happier with clean, restful sleep. And so will you if your baby is not fretful and overstimulated.

Adults who have lost awareness of their conscious connection to the higher realms also benefit greatly from a sound sleep. It is important to remember that connection to Source energy is never lost, it is the remembering of the connection that is forgotten. Sleep is the best opportunity to reconnect with the Source because, during rest, the body can be protected while the soul travels. If circumstances dictate that the body cannot find a safe place to rest itself, the person will likely experience ill health and supreme difficulty with emotional issues. It is in the safe sleep state that the body can heal itself most effectively. In a secure, hygienic sleep environment, the soul has the ability to connect directly with the Source energy during the dream state. It is during this time that the most intense healing occurs. As you become more consciously aware, you can meet with your spirit guides and direct the healing consciously.

Sleep has a dual purpose because the physical body is very precious and requires concerted rest too. Energetic healing of the corporal and spiritual body is most efficient during sleep. You cannot have a full earthly experience in an exhausted physical form.

Scientists have yet to reach consensus on exactly why the

body needs to sleep. We know that it just does. Our technology has advanced to the point that with abundant resources, we can feed and keep the body alive 24/7 without any break for sleep. Although the body's physical needs may be met, the consciousness of the true self struggles desperately. At the very least we go mad without breaking for sleep, suffering from all manner of emotional imbalances. This type of scenario, of course, is not sustainable. In fact, severe sleep deprivation is considered an inhumane act in modern society—a form of torture that ultimately leads to death of the material body. As a collective, we know that sleep deprivation is cruel, but we have not agreed on exactly why it is so profoundly detrimental to the body.

Here's what I know: The sleeping body is a conduit for the soul to reconnect with Source energy. Sleep allows the body to be at rest in a safe, secure environment while the energy body reconnects with its higher self. If the sleeping environment is sufficiently insecure or if there is paranoia about the safety of the physical body, the energy body cannot adequately connect with its Source. Without the connection to the universal Source, the energy body cannot revitalize itself. Lack of connection causes severe distress that is detrimental to the whole being. The physical body is revitalized by food and water. The energy body is revitalized by connecting with the universal life force. Even the densest of beings maintain this primordial connection, though they are ultimately unaware of it. Connecting with the Source is the most natural part of life.

When we are overworked and feeling overwhelmed, frequently the first thing to go is a good night's rest. We are delusional in thinking that doing more is better for us in the long run. Because of the ingrained push to work harder and longer, it is common to attempt to supplement the physical body's energy with herbs, medications, or stimulating substances, like caffeine, to keep it going. There is an unrelenting attempt to fit more into each day. Our priorities are so misaligned in this culture that we can even feel guilty when we rest and do nothing but attend to ourselves. We have embedded coping mechanisms into everyday life without even thinking about the impact it has on us. Other times when we are overworking, we cannot unwind sufficiently to fall asleep. Furthermore, if we're worrying, the mind's activity can cause insomnia.

Allow yourself to just *be* from time to time. Be unscheduled. Your physical body can only do so much. Instead of relentlessly trying to keep your body going, place the attention and effort toward addressing the energy body that has carried you through eternity. The idea of taking care of the whole self can be challenging when the whole being is not first acknowledged. That said, everyone is aware of the importance of sleep and rest on some level. This goes for both children and adults. Adequate sleep is essential for proper function of the whole being. The idea is to work consciously, not harder. And when the work is done, to relax, unwind, and rest. Being attuned to Source energy makes the conscious aspects of life possible.

You must take care of yourself before you can fully be present to take care of others. An overwhelmed mother is not the best mother to her children. The same is true for fathers.

An overworked employee is not the best operative in a business. With overworking, the probability of burnout and mistakes is one-hundred percent, as important things are inevitably forgotten, and the general attitude toward focusing on the workload suffers.

The better idea is to achieve some semblance of balance in life.

That said, balance for one person may not be the same as it is for another. What is consistent and universal is the need for plentiful, quality sleep. Balance cannot be attained if you are not getting the proper rest to align your soul with Source energy, or if the needs of your body are neglected and you are worn out emotionally or physically.

Most of the learning that occurs during the ascension process occurs during the hours of deep sleep. The actions to reinforce the lessons you receive will be executed during your waking hours. Moreover, it is imperative to recognize the dynamics between the energy body and the physical body if you want to cultivate your ability to elevate your frequency. A harmonious alignment with Source is ultimately required to transcend the third dimension.

CHAPTER 8

Balance

Achieving balance in our lives requires more than just eight to ten hours of restful sleep. Our bodies crave equilibrium between the physical self and the nonphysical self. Our souls need it if our energy is to ascend to higher frequencies.

The physical body is constantly moving toward physiologic balance, the state known as *homeostasis*. There are physical and environmental insults that can injure the body or contribute to its malfunctioning, but the condition of the energy body is more impactful. The energy body is highly intertwined with the physical body and influences the manifestation of its conditions, whether they be of sickness or health.

The energy body is in a constant state of motion to achieve energetic balance through proper alignment of its energy centers and the expansion of consciousness. Imbalances in the energy body will first affect you emotionally and then can manifest in the physical body disguised as infections, cancer, mental illness, and heart disease, for example. Energy balance, on the other hand, creates vibrancy and alertness. Your physical appearance and overall health are a direct reflection of your level of consciousness and whether your energy centers are aligned. It is entirely possible to lead a full life on the planet Earth in perfect health and free of disease. But it requires extreme vigilance of the whole self and awakening to consciousness to achieve.

I tend to think about my life like six slices of a pie. I have the career slice and the spiritual slice. I also have slices for the physical body, the mind, the significant other, and the family. My life pie never seemed to balance for most of my adulthood. Either I would have time and no money, or I would be working myself to death and have no meaningful relationships. I might have advanced my career but find myself blocked spiritually or somehow disconnected from nature. It always seemed like something had to give. Not only could I not have it all, but I couldn't achieve balance. I began to ask myself why the coveted balance was so elusive. It appeared attainable but at the same time always seemed just out of reach.

Until I began my conscious ascension process, I was going about achieving balance unconsciously. For instance, I might accept an intense job that was not aligned with my being just to earn a paycheck. This would appease my mind because it would not have to immediately worry about paying the bills. But in this construct, I never achieved balance because I would ultimately become stressed and unhappy in the job. The misalignment took me away from my family and left me little time for myself. In a job that was not aligned with my purpose, I also would be unfulfilled due to my inability to commune with nature or have satisfying relationships.

You see, everything is connected. If the core of me is unhappy, everything I touch is in some way ill fated.

In the past, I would try all sorts of tricks to project an image of happiness and balance. I would make sure I was dressed well and smiled on cue. I would race to get it all done. I would work extra hard to prove I was good enough, and at home, I would stretch myself to be a good mother and spouse. It seemed that everyone was taken care of: my employer, my child, and my spouse. Everyone except me. This behavior created resentment because so long as everyone else was satisfied, no one seemed to care about how I was doing. I hated that. There was never a day that I came home from work and dinner was already set on the table, all the laundry washed and folded, and my child bathed and cared for. Everyone was in suspended animation waiting for me to do those things for them. Regardless of how personal this scenario felt, I understood that this reliance on me did not come from a place of malice. They were just unconscious beings behaving unconsciously.

If you feel like your relationships are similarly imbalanced, then everyone around you is probably awake yet unconscious too. Everybody in our culture appears to be carrying too much and needs someone to shoulder some of the burdens. Everyone is in some way off balance. It ends up being the agilest and selfless who are left to pick up the pieces.

The unconscious approach to life was not working for me, but it served a purpose: It became the root of the unhappiness that led up to my awakening.

Work-family balance is often neglected for reasons of financial gain. As we discussed in the last chapter, the rigors of constant work are rewarded in many societies and overworking is seen as a sign of dedication and strength. In such a paradigm, there is little appreciation for the working individual's health and well-being. In this hyper-productive environment, family relationships suffer immensely and the person shouldering most of the burden often collapses. Women suffer from nervous exhaustion, fibromyalgia, and autoimmune disorders. Men drop dead of heart attacks.

Usually, to prevent a collapse in the short term, the overburdened individual drops something because no one can possibly carry it all. Over the long run, personal health suffers, as do relationships. This way of life leads to a perpetual imbalance that shows up as emotional and relationship strain and physical illness.

To lead a conscious life is to have a balanced lifestyle. Like life itself, balance is in a state of flux. It is a verb rather than a noun. Consciousness pushes you toward equilibrium because awareness is impossible with a mind that is preoccupied with getting everything done. Once you are open enough to attune to your true self, you will drop everything in your life that's unnecessary almost immediately. The shift will be felt on the deepest level of your being. You will stop thinking about doing it all to satisfy others and prioritize your obligations in support of yourself.

Unfortunately, for many people, it is a life-threatening illness that forces the shift. It will take a cancer diagnosis or a heart attack to finally wake a person up and mandate that they limit themselves to doing only that which is vitally important. For me, if you'll recall, I thought I had a brain tumor. Now I know how incredibly fortunate I was to wake up consciously before getting physically sick. It took me having the experience of multidimensional travel and getting fired from my job to really embrace the need to balance the contents of my existence.

When you are consciously aware and come into equilibrium, you will be amazed at what opens up for you. Within three months of losing my high-stress job, I lost thirty pounds and began to enjoy quality time with my son on a daily basis. I also spent meaningful time with my retiring parents and traveled to France where I started writing *The Duality of Being*. I opened an online store and moved to a beautiful new home in which I take pleasure residing. I could have never accomplished a quarter of the initiatives I have pursued in the past few years had I remained stressed and burned out in an unconscious state. The most important thing that occurred for me after my big shift into consciousness was to find balance. Within three months, I felt better than I had in two decades.

The most important thing I did to find my equilibrium was to trust myself. It takes a lot of courage to trust in the power of the Universe because we are unconscious to its power. In the race to get it all done by the end of the day, it's easy to become oblivious to the multitude of miracles occurring in every moment. As I awoke, I had to learn to trust that I would be supported. I did this by reminding myself several times a day that I was okay, honestly okay. There is an order to everything, and I surrendered to this order.

At times, I would become afraid like my past self would become, worrying about this or that. But I committed to not worrying, as I'd realized by then that it is always a choice to worry. A negative situation might be brewing, but it was my choice whether to worry about it. Moreover, I could make decisions about what to do in the face of a potentially worrying situation. For me, the release breathing (see Chapter 4, "Elevating Your Frequency") helped. When I need to restore my equilibrium, I chose to focus on my breath, feel my feelings, and remind myself as many times as needed that I am supported. That everything is fine. What was really bothering me were memories of my past before my conscious awakening. It is the mind that worries, and I was not going to be held hostage by the mind any longer.

The key to finding truth and knowing flatly that everything is all right is to be present in the moment. When you are present at the very moment you are asking for peace and equilibrium, you can see that you are, in fact, just fine. It is when you dwell upon past situations that did not turn out as you had hoped, or you look toward the uncertainty of the future that fear sets into the mind. You must remember that the past is no longer here. It is only the memory and feelings of the past that persist. And the future will always be a mystery that unfolds from the actions of the now.

A mature mind knows that the unknowns of the future are not to be feared, they are to be revered for their majestic unfolding. You must let go of all doubt and imagine as many possibilities as conceivable for your future. Think big. Think very BIG. Once you are conscious, these possibilities will become available to you, as well as many others you cannot yet comprehend. It is your highly resonating energetic frequency that allows the greatest possibilities to materialize.

To achieve the coveted balance, you simply must learn to operate in harmony with the force of the Universe. Although this once-elusive balance leads to sustained happiness, it is crucial to understand that balance is not one and done. There always remains the constant of change in our life circumstances, therefore the need to perpetually rebalance exists. Each rebalancing does not have to be as onerous as the initial balance. It can be thought of as a process like fine-tuning an instrument. Life is in constant motion. The interplay that feels like the source of equilibrium today will invariably change tomorrow. The key is to be attuned in an ongoing manner to the sometimes-subtle changes occurring within you as well as to changes in the environments that are a part of the greater context of your existence. Allow all the bending and flexing necessary to lead an overall happy and balanced life.

If you feel that you were called to read this book, then I believe all of humanity needs you to be balanced and conscious. Many sentient beings around the world are depending on you. Just like me, you have your own children, immediate family, friends, and colleagues who are influenced by your conscious awareness. The Earth itself is in dire need of humanity to be conscious to assist it in raising its frequency. Balance is a crucial aspect of the ascension process because only a wholly balanced being can pursue his or her rightful path.

CHAPTER 9

A Circuitous Path

When I was thirty-five years old, I attempted to take my own life. I was on my chosen path of becoming a cardiothoracic surgeon when it turned out that I simply couldn't do it anymore. A major shift had occurred within me. I could not explain at the time, but I knew it was time for me to leave my surgical career behind me forever.

I don't remember the exact date, but I remember that it was a Friday. For some reason, the timing doesn't seem to matter. I can think of a hundred reasons why I wanted to leave Earth: everything from sleep deprivation, exhaustion, loneliness, and general unhappiness, to financial stress. It really was for none of these reasons that I decided to leave. I knew the physical stresses I was experiencing were temporary. In the larger scheme of things, I thought the work and sacrifice I was putting in was indeed worth the opportunity to train as a heart surgeon. Despite the rationalization of my mind, there was a trigger that I couldn't exactly put my finger on. It was much deeper than any single immediate challenge.

I was working every day in the Cardiovascular Intensive Care Unit (CVICU) as a clinical fellow. I must say that on many levels it was the most meaningful year I ever experienced while practicing medicine. It felt like I was finally on the right track. I loved what I was learning even though the work was arduous and the hours very long. The fellows would have one twenty-four-hour period off per month. That meant, for one day a month, you would not be paged to procure organs for transplant or be expected in the hospital for surgical rounds. All other days you were on, even if just to attend the morbidity and mortality conference or complete clinical rounds on Saturday mornings. I worked very hard at learning to manage my critical patients as well as learning surgical techniques unique to CT surgery. I was getting along well with my colleagues and mentors, and I had a good relationship with the nurses in the CVICU. I felt I had come a long way to be able to achieve the milestone of becoming a female surgeon.

In my personal life, I was single and felt very isolated. I did not have much of a social life. I had some friends, but not many close relationships. I was instead entirely dedicated to my work. I would get up at 4:45 A.M. every weekday to be on rounds in the CVICU at 0600 hours sharp (we used military time to keep time in the hospital). There was no telling how late I would make it home most evenings. I stayed overnight in the hospital on call every third night.

At the hospital, I shared an on-call room with my colleagues. In this on-call room were a desk with a computer, a single bed, several small lockers, and a small bathroom. We affectionately called this space the *bunker*. It is where we fellows slept when on call and where we congregated during the day between our surgical cases. In the on-call room, we would empty our white coats of unused syringes, sutures, and other medications, like lidocaine, pouring them into an innocuous container. There was a collection of such items sitting on the shelf above the desk, in a small emesis basin. You know, one of those kidney-shaped plastic dishes that are given to bedridden patients when they need to vomit.

One Friday evening, I picked up a vial of idly dropped succinylcholine, a paralyzing anesthetic, along with a needle and syringe from that small basin in the bunker. That same evening after work, still in my scrubs, I drove along the Pacific Coast Highway to my favorite spot overlooking the ocean. I was driving my leased C-class Mercedes Benz that I had gifted myself on my thirty-third birthday. I parked on top of a small hill, away from other cars that would enter the unpaved parking lot below. I watched the sunset with one of my beloved CDs playing softly in the background. When I decided it was time to die, I crawled in the back seat and drew up the syringe of succinylcholine, plucking at the filled syringe to free all the air bubbles. I thought I should inject it quickly so that I would get the entire vial in before I became incapacitated.

I felt a little fear of the unknown in that moment, but otherwise, I felt relatively calm. I hadn't really planned how it would go and didn't overthink anything. I didn't think that I would be leaving anything behind. I did not feel like there was anyone I should call, and I did not prepare a note of any kind. I hadn't thought through what would become of my body. I didn't seem to care about that. I had felt that life held no more surprises for me and that I was just done living. I didn't feel particularly sad or even melancholy. Just empty.

I readied myself by getting comfortable in the back seat. I thought I would just lay down and die. I used my right hand to inject the anesthetic into a prominent vein in the middle of my left inner arm. The access was easy. I injected the full vial but not before feeling the beginnings of paralysis setting in. Almost immediately, I felt my muscles stiffen and harden with rigor. The muscles in my chest and abdomen tightened to the point where I could move only a teaspoon of air with each respiration. As panic set in, I began to focus on the music playing in the background. I was reassured when I realized I would be able to hear until the very end. My neck felt like it was stuck in a twisted position and I could not move my head at all. I had turned to stone. At that moment, I realized that I wasn't ready to go, and I became afraid.

As I was gasping for what I thought were my last breaths, I heard my inner self speak to me, I believe, for the very first time. Inside, I said, *I'm sorry, this is so stupid. I'm so sorry.* I fought for a minute eternity before I would begin to regain my breath. Moments later, I could feel my hardened muscles beginning to soften. Over the next few seconds, I could move and take deeper breaths. Most of my muscle function resumed to normal rather quickly but my eye muscles took a bit longer. I lay there in the back seat recovering quietly and thinking.

Before I knew it, it was the dark of night and, to my surprise, I saw a bright flashlight looking inside my car windows. I hadn't noticed but a police patrol car had arrived, and a cop was checking on me. I rolled down my window and said that I was fine, that I had just fallen asleep admiring the sunset. The officer seemed receptive to this explanation and was on his way.

When he was gone, I started up my car and slowly drove away. I stopped at a grocery store and grabbed a deli sandwich on my way back. I decided to check into a hotel room that night. Early the next morning, I put my scrubs on and headed back to the hospital for morning rounds.

That whole day, I felt sublime happiness. I was peaceful inside because I now knew what I had to do: I needed to leave my career behind and get on my rightful path. I was not sure exactly where that rightful path was leading me, but I knew it needed to be a drastic change from where I had been. I didn't tell anyone of the prior night's ordeal. In fact, I never mentioned it to anyone, not ever, until writing this description of events. I was too afraid of being judged. To write this book about my evolution into consciousness, I decided I had to come clean and share my entire journey—the triumphs as well as the falls.

You see, life is complicated, and we may do many regrettable, painful things along the way. No one is awake and conscious for an entire lifespan. Consciousness is something that is revealed by the entwined passageways of a life fraught with pain and introspection.

Please know, your past actions, however misguided or malignant, in no way preclude you from attaining enlightenment. There is always time to get back on your rightful path. Each of us will have several opportunities to correct our path during a single embodiment. If the final correction is not made due to free will, we will reincarnate to have another chance to reach conscious awareness and elevate the frequency of our energy body.

My entire medical career was a chosen path. Although I embarked upon it because of my free will, it was not on my rightful path. Becoming a surgeon just seemed like the right thing to do at the time. I was looking for a purpose and a medical career seemed rather purposeful. A wise friend once told me that just because you can do something doesn't mean you should do it. I have never forgotten this.

After I quit my fellowship at the hospital, I cried for three days straight. It wasn't something I wanted to do, it was something I had to do. The call for change sounded from deep within. I still think back on that time in my life fondly. I am very grateful to have had the opportunity to practice clinical medicine. I experienced tremendous learning about the human condition and this ultimately created the opening for me to find my true purpose. Traveling your rightful path means heeding the call of the soul and bringing purpose and joy into your life.

Our souls are embodied so that we can have a full experience of human life. Being human is as much about having physical experiences as it is about perfecting the internal soul.

The pursuit of a life purpose advances the soul's maturation process. It is essential. Feeling and working through the emotions of the energy body is equally essential. Some people need to be driven to attempt suicide while others need to be riddled with cancer before they will wake up and begin the inward journey of soul work. The passage of introspection serves as the ultimate guide to find their rightful purpose. Our life purpose was contracted before we were born. We agreed to the terms of the embodied life we assumed. There were no mistakes and the experiences were designed to teach us the lessons necessary for soul evolution. At birth, we all forget why we came here. We carry on in ignorance until the emotional burden of unconsciousness is too heavy to carry any further.

Regardless of how individual awakenings occur, an immediate change in perspective about life ensues. When they finally wake up, people will focus on doing what they have always wanted to do. The journey in life no longer is about the accrual of money, credentials, or material objects. Life now is about fulfilling their soulful purpose for being alive. A soul's reason for embodiment may be to learn about forgiveness, to overcome the ego mind and illusion of the physical body, or to serve humanity is some momentous way. There are souls that have reincarnated to complete a task that was left undone in a previous existence. There are as many reasons to live as there are embodied lives. The purpose of your soul's incarnation on Earth can be found in your soul contract that is accessible through dedicated introspection along the path of conscious awareness. Changing direction or vocation doesn't mean that your original path was a bad path or a waste of time. The path you chose before awakening just might not be your rightful path—the path your soul intends for you to ultimately take during this incarnation. Ironically, sometimes the threat of death is exactly what is needed to wake up and truly live the life you designed before incarnating. Waking up is required to finally hear the voice of the higher self and to be what it is you are meant to be.

When I learn of a suicide through social media or in the headline news, a part of me quietly understands why the person did it. I get it on a personal level. I am in no position to judge another for the decision to take his or her life. What I do know is that making the difficult decision to die is in no way easy or hasty. It often stems from a lifetime of searching for external validation and fulfillment when true actualization comes from within. It is difficult for us to make sense of people's attempts to end their lives when they are at the height of their worldly achievements, or when outwardly they seem to have everything anyone could ever want—loving partners, children, status, influence, creative work, money, fame, you name it. But contrary to belief, it is often at the moment of highest accomplishment that a profound sadness sets in when we realize that the hard work and struggle we've endured to achieve the success has not fulfilled us. The soul can feel empty despite the worldly trappings of success.

All the fame and fortune in the world cannot appease the yearning of the soul. The inner self demands attention and always beckons to be heard. If we neglect the call of the soul, it cannot be actualized on Earth. At a certain point, the life energy within us will choose to shed its outer shell (that which we call the body) and leave Earth so it may heal itself and find another suitable existence for further maturation. The body does not want to die. The physical body fights for its survival. It is the soul that chooses to depart. Without higher consciousness, the body is no more than decaying flesh and bone.

We are mistaken as a collective conscience to believe that labels like *depression* and *hopelessness* sum up the experience of a soul that has departed via suicide. The rationale for the departure lies much deeper than we can perceive, and I suspect this is why suicide creates such great confusion among onlookers. When a successful, famous, or affluent person commits suicide, society is left dumbfounded and perplexed. We have a hard time imagining what possibly could be *wrong* in the context of having every physical desire and need met. In our moments of reflection and compassion, we often wonder what the problem could be if an individual has achieved great wealth and success. We must come to understand that neither money, success, or fame, nor any material possession, has the power to appease the soul.

Suicide is happening at an alarming rate in the world today among veterans returning from war, teenagers, medical professionals, and in the mainstream adult population too. The medical community has yet figured out that no amount or variety of pharmaceutical drugs can heal an ailing soul. Our psychiatric medicines only numb the mind to the pain of the emotional body. If we believe we are effectively treating mental or emotional problems through these methods, we are sorely mistaken. Healing the soul occurs on an energetic level and it requires the persistent work of conscious introspection from the individual who is labeled as depressed. The individual must be willing to do the work. If professionals in modern medicine today were true healers, they would first address the energetic, emotional body before prescribing drugs or surgically treating the body. The most remarkable advancements in medicine will come from this understanding.

CHAPTER 10

The Root of Happiness

Happiness doesn't come from a place or the possession of things. Happiness doesn't come from relationships or careers. It comes from within. True happiness is a state of being that comes from alignment with your higher self and an attunement with the rhythm of the Universe. Physical objects like cars, clothing, and jewels are all false "idols" when it comes to happiness; they rarely bring us the rewards we expect them to deliver. We worship material items and cash in our culture. Coveted things, of course, may incite temporary satisfaction but in themselves, they do not possess the essence of pure happiness. And the same is true of careers, relationships, and even our children. These things can be the enablers of fulfillment but in themselves do not generate the happiness within you. Similarly, many have found themselves working in the *perfect* job only to be devoid of fulfillment and true happiness.

Happiness is a transient state of being. Like other emotions, happiness comes and goes. Even if we should find alignment with the true self and completely surrender to the Source of all that *is*, there will be moments when we do not feel happy. We will still be challenged with lessons in life. As human beings, we are called to clear emotional blocks and release our deep-rooted fears. We will never complete our souls' evolutionary work. Instead, we will continue to learn and release over a multitude of incarnations spanning many eons.

It is perfectly acceptable and okay not to feel happy all the time. We experience many emotions which all play important roles in our soulful awakening. Once the source of happiness is known, you can always return there. And you can look forward to the time when you will no longer look to physical things to bring you happiness. It can be liberated at any time and in any situation if you allow it to arise.

Happiness can appear and disappear at a moment's notice. Different things facilitate happiness in different people at different times. Things or events can be infused with the high energy of happiness, but the feeling of happiness is generated from within. We have all witnessed someone crying at a party or have felt sad on what should be a joyous occasion. We have all experienced dissatisfaction and regret from purchases. No matter how attached we feel to certain objects, people, and experiences, they are not the source of happiness.

In truth, happiness is something you can feel for simply being alive, for having cool water to drink on a hot day, or upon smelling a single rose. The feeling of happiness comes from having a sense of abundance and knowing that you are enough. A happy feeling is the antithesis of the pursuit of more. It is a feeling that comes from being present and being grateful for what you *do* have. It is not from expecting more in the future or regretting what you didn't have in the past.

It took me four decades to find the kind of happiness that now radiates from within me. I am not speaking of the sort of temporary satisfaction that comes from acquiring things or achieving material success. I'm not referring to laughter provoked by comedians. I am talking about the sustained happiness that is inherent in the soul of my being. If I remember I am in tune with my higher self and connected to Source energy, there is happiness. I now experience spontaneous laughter from deep within my soul and no longer feel the lingering depths of sadness I once did.

PART TWO

Human Constructs to Transcend

On the ascension path, we become acquainted with the nonphysical higher self that is the eternal part of our dual nature. In the process of letting go of limiting beliefs about our identity and capabilities, we realize that some of the institutions we cling to on Earth 3.0 do not exude universal truths. There are many pervasive ideals on the planet, which have varying degrees of benevolence. In Part Two, "Human Constructs to Transcend," we shall discuss the institutions on Earth that will no longer serve you once you travel outside of the third dimension.

Remember, leaving the third dimension can occur during the night in your dream state or at the final separation of your life energy from the body at the moment of complete cellular death.

Human constructs are theories and ideologies that exist only in the minds of people. They are not relevant in the broader context of existence. Four primary constructs are thriving on Earth today. These prevailing constructs are time, money, race, and religion. Theories of how things should be or should work in the physical realm are not universal truths in the Multiverse.

Constructs do not exist in the absence of human beings. They are theories and paradigms that change and shift over the centuries to suit those who are in the highest seats of power. They are ideologies designed to manage populations, appease doubting hearts, and questioning minds. The danger of some constructs is that they are harmful to still-unconscious people who do not know there is more to life than the delusions of humanity.

CHAPTER 11

Time

Time, as we understand it, is a human construct of perception. The measure and counting of time in the way we measure and count it with clocks and calendars is somewhat arbitrary. Given that humankind is not the only group of conscious beings in existence, these concepts of time have only limited utility. Humans populate a unique planet in an infinite, expanding Multiverse. The construct of time works here because we have mandated it by consensus. It frames our perceptions and categorizes the lives of everything we bring into existence.

It is difficult to conceive that time does not exist. Most people have never really thought about it. It is the foundation of all that ever has happened, is happening, and will happen. All things in our minds are in some way measured in terms of linear time. It is how we keep track of our affairs and how we reference our remembering.

We have a linear way of rationalizing and arranging events in our minds. The time construct of past, present, and future supports the perception of linear-based thinking and is fundamental to how we process life experiences. The time construct also helps us in cataloging our memories. The linear aspect of life happenings is, however, only a perception we imbue our lives with due to our perpetually unconscious state.

Timelines in the broader context of existence are not linear but converging. Universal timelines intersect and are not experienced in the linear construct that we imagine. Past, present, and future are all existing at once and separated only by a single moment. The intersection of past, present, and future is in the *now* moment. The now is not static but in perpetual motion. As humans, we perceive time passing because of memories and perceptions as our bodies grow and then decay. We also have a convention of labeling time on the X-axis of the graphic below (see figure below). It would be more useful to consider time on the Y-axis, where all timelines converge on the single point we call *Now*.

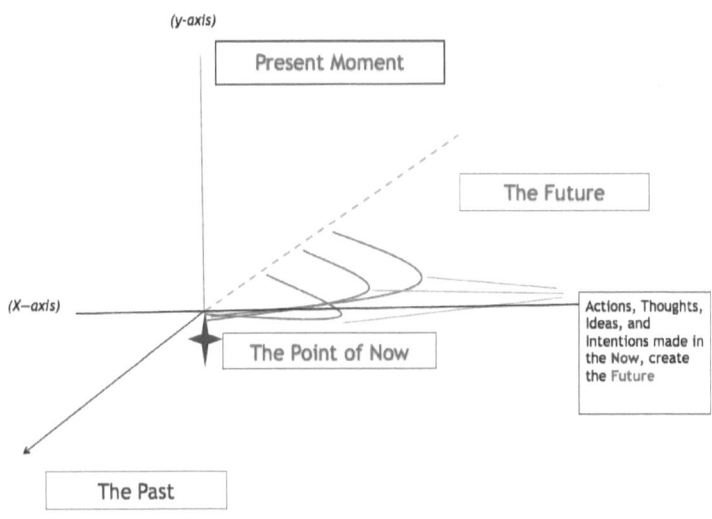

Metaphysical Point of Now diagram.
Created by Susan Nicholas, MD. 2017

Metaphysical diagram of Time and the Point of Now.

The past, present, and future converge from moment to moment. Your future is converging on your present in every moment of your existence. Similarly, your present is converging on your past in every moment. The future unfolds moment by moment through the power of your intentions, thoughts, and ideas in the present. The future is put into motion by the actions taken in the now. The past is essentially the future that has already passed through the point of now. The convergence of timelines in the Universe is antithetical to how we conceptualize time in the third dimension.

What's the basis of Earth time? Let's begin by looking at the unit of measure of time: the second. Since the relatively recent institution of the atomic clock in 1967, we have accepted that one second is equivalent to the duration of 9,192,631,770 periods of the radiation corresponding to the transition between the two hyperfine levels of the ground state of the cesium 133 atoms at 0 degrees Kelvin (K).[1] The "cesium second" was defined in 1967 from an esteemed 1958 physics proof.[2] This is the base unit of time measurement accepted today by the collective human consensus. The radiation transition of the cesium 133 atom is the basis by which we understand what is past, present, and future. There exists a strontium clock with even greater accuracy of the measurement of a second than the atomic cesium clock. I wonder what is the point of measuring something that does not exist with greater accuracy? The measurement of time is a revered and celebrated scholarly occupation of the time construct.

Imagine that it is not time that exists, but rather the measurement of a second that exists. Or better yet, the measurement of a radiation wave of a cesium or strontium atom. We have figured out a way to measure the transition of radiation fields of atomic particles and call this measure *a second*. Though an extraordinary feat, the time construct, as we know it, is nothing more than that.

When we turn our attention to larger divisions of time, the calendars have their own secular and religious histories. Calendars were used to normalize planting and harvesting cycles and to standardize religious holidays. In the West, the Julian calendar was first implemented by Julius Caesar in 46 B.C.E. and replaced by the Gregorian calendar in 1582 C.E. by Pope Gregory XIII. The use of either the Julian or modern Gregorian calendar over the past 2,000-plus years is recent when compared to the generally accepted age of the Earth: approximately 4.55 billion years. The formal quantification of Earth's age was informed by the scientific understanding of the planet's physical properties. These properties include isotopes, their radioactive decay, and geologic observations.[3]

Contemplate further the vastly intangible energetic component of Earth's existence. Our human incarnation might provide a useful comparison to Earth's life experience, as the planet is very much alive. One could concede that Earth is having a period of third-dimensional physicality much like we are. We know that it has undergone remarkable evolutions during this present 3D existence. It would stand to reason that the exact age of the Earth is as infinite as the Source energy that created it.

I've often wondered: If the time construct is real, why we must always be reminded of it? Why does the quality of some minutes differ from that of others? When we are experiencing high-frequency emotions, like love and passion, the minutes seem to disappear without notice, freely detached in their permanence. Those same minutes in instances of great anticipation or pain are unhurried in their passing, personifying the deftness of an eternity.

The experience of time passing is an energetic expression of Earth's life force, a distinctive quality of our home planet. But only the physical form is marked by the passing of time on Earth. This tedious wonder is not carried over into the beyond.

It is not wrong to have a time construct. It is indeed useful in everyday life. What tends to confuse people is how to process cosmic events occurring outside of the construct. Because most people do not have an awareness of what goes on outside of Earth, accepting the construct is easy. Conscious beings, however, know that when the energy body leaves 3D reality, time is distorted, and the construct dissipates instantaneously. The energy body will perceive itself as spending *hours* in an alternate dimension engaging in events that on Earth would consume an entire day. However, on the jaunt back to Earth, you find that you've only been gone for seven or eight minutes. Energy is significantly slower in the third dimension. It is this distortion that has compelled me to ponder the very existence of time.

Beings existing at higher dimensions don't share our construct of time. There is only the now.

Should death be your first and possibly final separation from the physical, expect that you will never again have to ask, "What time is it?" You will become oblivious to the construct with the realization that now is the only time that has ever been. Timeliness has no station on the path unwinding infinity and urgency no purpose.

CHAPTER 12

Money

During my childhood, there never seemed to be enough money, and happy feelings surrounding money were largely absent. Money was commonly lacking, and no one that I knew had much of it. I used to earn $2 a week in allowance during the late 1970s. I always thought this cash was very precious despite my habit of spending it on my favorite little red Swedish fish candy. I had to do numerous chores to earn that money, and it had long held negative connotations for me. Both of my parents worked full-time jobs and yet they still did not bring in enough income to raise a family of five children comfortably. As I look back on my life, riches never flowed freely to me. I acquired capital through tireless efforts spanning most days and nights. Growing up poor is a common reason why many people hold onto limiting beliefs surrounding money for their entire lifetime.

Limiting beliefs can include ideas like *Money does not grow on trees* or *There is never enough money*. In circumstances of scarcity, we embody feelings of fear, worry or even shame around the idea of money. If we want more money but have underlying beliefs related to lack, these beliefs can prevent us from acquiring wealth. Money, like all things on Earth, is a form of energy. It is a construct we have created to signify wealth, and it often carries the energy signature of abundance. When we have negative emotions or feelings about money, we express the energy of lack and do not attract the higher frequency possibilities that provide abundant resources. Releasing limiting beliefs about money is like releasing any other heavy, negative emotion. That energy of lack must be transmuted into the higher-frequency feelings of worthiness and self-confidence if we are to attract greater means or higher incomes. You must have the same confidence in yourself that you have in the Universe's capacity to provide if you are to transcend the money construct entirely. The universal energy is an infinite and intelligent one that feels your true emotional resonance. You must have implicit confidence in yourself to break through the lifelong limiting beliefs and patterns of past thinking with their related emotions. Having faith in yourself begins with accepting that you are enough, just as you are, and that abundance is your divine right.

Have you ever looked at your bank account balance only to feel fear or a sense of panic? This fear comes from the mind's belief that you will not be able to pay a bill or make ends meet at the end of the month. As human beings, we give our power to money and ignore entirely that the power of creation is within us. Telling you that money is yet another illusion of the third dimension doesn't remove the fear of embarrassment or failure associated with not having enough. Our financial system creates annoying consequences and headaches when there is not enough money. Many people feel frustrated with money because it does not seem to flow consistently or at the right times. There may be more month at the end of your money. Someone who owes you money could fail to come through with it on time, or unplanned expenses can cause grief. The sudden need to repair a computer or a car may disturb the balance of your fragile finances. These circumstances feel very real when you are going through them, making the situations appear out of your control.

When the money doesn't add up, there is an imbalance. Money problems are a result of internal energetic imbalances where we say we need more but harbor the dense energy of lack at the same time. Everything must balance. Any gross asymmetry in life will need to move toward correction. Restoring financial equilibrium requires changing your energy signal when it comes to money. When dense, negative feelings emerge from your heart center or solar plexus in response to thoughts about finances, you must ask your higher self why you feel this way. Your heart center may be radiating feelings of frustration or hate in response to a critical capital situation. The solar plexus, which sits in the center of your body just below the rib cage, may generate the feeling of doom that pains you in the pit of your stomach, perhaps causing you to lose your appetite in the face of financial stress. Your mind will give you a hundred justifications and tell you that it is foolish even to ask, but you need to clarify with your higher self what precisely is going on inside of you. Why is the pain so deep and why are the patterns repeating themselves?

Throughout my life, I would experience feast or famine patterns surrounding money. I would have gainful employment only to be laid off or have an employer who couldn't pay me regularly. I often found myself in precarious financial situations and never believed I was well compensated. I felt insecure financially and couldn't figure out why repeatedly, I was experiencing unstable work scenarios. I would become angry and frustrated, and at times wished that money didn't exist at all. When I looked back on these situations, my initial thoughts were that I was unlucky or cursed in some way. I always felt terrible about myself during difficult financial times too. I perceived the situations as happening to me and believed that I did not have any control over my predicament. I didn't realize that my feelings were dictating the financial scenarios I experienced in life and that I was giving my power away to money.

To get to the root of your feelings about money, you must be honest with yourself. Many money imbalances are rooted in childhood experiences where you believe you are not enough or are undeserving. The emotions surrounding money issues that you grew up with are still within you unless you have actively cleared them. Limiting beliefs like *I don't deserve more money* may be surviving in the deepest recesses of the soul. You must fully release those limiting beliefs to reclaim your energy.

The next time you feel stressed about money, hold the stressed feeling in awareness and ask yourself from where it is coming. Reveal the origin of the dense feelings using your inner voice. Feel the pounding of your heart. If it is pounding with anxiety, breathe through the discomfort, holding your attention on your breath. Narrow your thoughts to just two words: in and out. The purpose of focusing on the breath is to consciously move past the heavy feelings and replace them with a sense of calm.

Once you are calm, tell yourself that you are remembering and now releasing the memories and beliefs surrounding money that is holding you back. At this moment, ask the higher self what you can do to alleviate the situation. In a relaxed manner, you can also begin to create affirmations to assist you should these feeling arise again. For example, you might say to yourself

"I am more powerful than any situation presented to me" or "I am in control of how I react in all financial situations." Make a habit of writing down your affirmations and rehearse them until they are automatic. Remind yourself as many times as necessary that *I am ok* and that *The money construct does not dictate my survival*. If your bank balance is creating discomfort, look at your bank account balance with gratitude, no matter what the number is. Tell yourself that the current amount is only temporary on your journey toward abundance. Each step you take to change your feelings and reactions surrounding money moves you forward along the path of conscious awareness.

Stay aware of how your feelings are changing during the introspective process. As you reconcile a belief and release it, replace it with a new, higher frequency understanding about money, such as knowing *Money is a form of energy*, and *There is more than enough money in the world to go around*. Reaffirm that all your needs are met with speed and grace. Ask the Universe to surprise you with its infinite possibilities to serve you. Always remember who you are. You are a child of God, eternally connected to the Source of all that *is*. You have an inalienable right to happiness and abundance.

Without a doubt, money can be a difficult construct to overcome. Living in a world where everything cost, we have created a need for cash to secure our physical survival. I needed an Ah-ha moment to conquer the money construct. When I thought back on the other human constructs, they were relatively more natural to let go of than the money construct. Race, for example, was easy to release because I knew I was a child of the Source, just as we all are, regardless of my skin color or gender. I knew I wasn't less capable or less intelligent because of my physical body. Race never really made sense to me so letting it go during my awakening was effortless.

Religion wasn't too difficult for me to release either because I never found the answer to what ailed my soul from any religious teaching or institution. My questions never answered, my soul purpose never revealed. Once I found I could trust and rely on my higher self, I no longer needed religion to comfort or explain things to me. Conscious awareness wholly dissolved the religious construct for me.

Regarding linear time, the idea of a time construct was a mere abstraction to me until I began traveling out-of-body. It wasn't until writing this manuscript that I truly conceptualized all of perceived time converging on a single moment we call *now*. After that, releasing the time construct was not difficult.

The money construct, however, had been elaborately intertwined in my physical being, yielding control over my emotions and well-being. At times I have been powerless in its wake, feeling high or low depending on its abundance or lack in my presence. Knowing money is a construct was not enough. Understanding that a lack of funds was related to my childhood beliefs of unworthiness was still not enough to release the hold the money construct had on me. You see, overcoming limiting beliefs is not intellectual. It is not just about knowing, it is about feeling.

I searched my soul for the roots I would someday pull to release this illusionary, thorny entanglement. Then it occurred to me, how I could remain vibrationally high when my funds were low. How to not panic in the face of uncertainty. I finally understood how to release the money construct forever.

In several worldly economies, we are taught to value net

worth. We are versed in saving money, investing, and responsible spending. The social commentary that boasts celebrity net worth and anecdotal tales of bankrupt millionaires inundates our news cycle. We are often confused when someone who is financially prosperous loses all his money, becomes depressed, or intoxicated with drugs. The confusion persists because we attach financial net worth to happiness and our self-worth, despite these things being unrelated. As a society, we emotionally connect our net worth to our self-esteem. Thereby, when we don't have money, we feel small and unimportant. On the contrary, in the presence of sufficient wealth, we tend to feel energized and empowered. In this paradigm, we can never indeed be financially free.

    A person is not financially free if when destitute, he feels insignificant, no more so than when rich, he feels superior. Understandably, we will have different feelings in situations of plenty and lack. However, no amount of money can ever define the self-worth of a perfect human-being connected to the Source of all that *is*. You may feel upset in a given situation, but to feel down on yourself due to finances keeps you from realizing your prize. If your emotions about yourself fluctuate depending on money, you are not yet financially free. In a situation of financial lack, we must remember that the way we feel inside is the frequency we resonate out to the Universe. The language of the Universe is the frequency of our feelings. When we feel bad about ourselves, we cannot overcome financial lack because we resonate a low frequency related to the belief that we are not enough. When the Universe picks up on your frequency of lack, it returns earthly circumstances that appear equally inadequate.

    We must resonate the highest confidence in ourselves,

irrespective of a bank account balance or financial situation, to achieve economic freedom. Real financial freedom is being emotionally free of the trappings of the money construct. Having self-confidence comes from knowing without a shadow of a doubt that you are enough and the power to create your abundance lies within you, and always has.

I overcame the illusion of the money construct when I realized that I could feel great inside regardless of my financial statements. I practiced being calm and confident in every funding situation knowing within me that the Universe fully supports me and that I am resourceful enough to support myself. Before my conscious awakening, I believed an employer had to pay me my worth and that I could not create it myself. In that mindset, I never felt that I received my fair value. When I finally woke up, I realized those financial patterns I had experienced were due to my belief that I was not capable or deserving enough to have what I wanted. I needed to embrace the fact that the power to earn and to live a life that I loved was always inside of me.

Every person born onto the Earth has a gift. We all have something miraculous within us that is designed to sustain us in life. We have also collectively created a money construct. In this paradigm, each of our innate gifts can be monetized to create financial wealth and overall abundance in life. Life challenges each of us to uncover our unique gift through the process of introspection. Once we find our true purpose, we realize that we never have to do long or hard work to create wealth and abundance. In the vibrational place of intention and awareness, the opportunity to entirely disconnect self-worth from financial net worth arises.

On my conscious journey, I learned to awaken myself during

those times that I would reflexively feel worthless by acknowledging my internal resistance to energy flow. It was those heavy feelings that were holding me back from my abundance. You see, thoughts are powerful, but emotions are even more so because it is your feelings that project into the universal substrate creating earthly scenarios and physical manifestations. The Universe hears the frequency of your feelings and provides for you accordingly. My Ah-ha moment was when I realized I could transform the low-frequency emotions of lack and worthlessness into the higher-frequency feelings of self-confidence and gratitude. I had to reprogram my thinking to learn to feel grateful for all that life was showing me. I finally realized that my physical reality was only a mirror of my internal feelings and beliefs. If I perceived something wrong with the unfolding of my reality, then I had to correct my emotional, vibrational state to see any meaningful changes in my physical existence. By saying to myself that I am infinitely more significant than any circumstance Earth-school can show me, that I decide how I react and feel around money, and that I am enough, was my energetic release. I now know that no person or thing can make me feel any way I do not want to feel. I am now confident in the higher order universal law of manifestation.

As you awaken to the myth of the money construct, repeat affirmations as many times as necessary to reprogram your thinking and feelings. You will begin to notice that feelings will continue to arise within you until they no longer need to be felt. Feelings no longer need to be felt once they transform through understanding and conscious awareness. Interrupt every dense feeling and behavior that no longer serves you or the Universe with conscious awareness. Notice how you begin to feel. Old, troublesome scenarios now have little to no effect on you. Know that the universal law is infinite and perfect. It is up to each of us to trust and then harness it to reveal our highest potential.

The Illusion

Money in our society today consists of pieces of paper, pressed metals, and electronic currencies. Money is not real. It is a form of exchange humans created to assign a value to the things we want to trade. It is an elaborate delusion that, in abundance, symbolizes wealth and prosperity.

When it comes to money, know that you never have to worry about it. Worrying is always a choice. Whatever the situation, you can decide to worry about it or not. The circumstance remains as it is either way. It is how you feel about the situation that ultimately transforms it. Ask yourself how or where you can get the money you need. Ask from your heart what you should do. Listen to your inner voice. The true self will communicate with you through your heart center, and it is all-knowing.

It sounds simplistic to say, "Don't worry" or "Let go of limiting thoughts." Does the mere act letting go of limiting thoughts pay the bills? No, of course not. Collectively we have created a lifestyle that costs. Nothing that the Earth willingly provides us is free anymore in our modern civilization. It is not that releasing dense energy pays the bills. It is the openings that are created by releasing heavy feelings that will bring in new possibilities that pay the bills. When we harbor limiting beliefs, we cut ourselves off from receiving higher frequency possibilities. Do not give pieces of paper or electronic figures on a screen power over you.

Mind The Gap

When we need money, we need it now. In the process of transforming emotions to align with the energy signature of abundance, we can feel doubt because of the seemingly slow pace of forming a new reality. This scenario is a typical example of the gap between the old patterns and the life we were living and the new frequency and patterns we are expanding toward. When the money needed does not materialize when the rent is due, for example, it is not surprising that the mind will want to panic as it relives past experiences. In a situation like this, it is helpful to exercise your power to decide how you are going to react. Instead of the tired feelings of panic that might involve avoidance, anger or fear, in its place decide to hold off on the emotional reaction, even if for just forty-eight hours. Decide that you are not going to go there emotionally this time around and suspend your usual actions for two days. In that time, imagine another outcome, something that you would love to happen instead. Tell yourself a different story, remembering the power of your thoughts and language. What could occur that would be in your highest good and the highest good of all others involved? When the rent is coming due, and the money isn't yet available, change your thinking to a best-case scenario like *I now have all the cash I need to pay my rent in-full and on-time*, remembering at every turn to remind yourself that you are enough. Elevated awareness about money will also impact your language and conversations around finances.

An exercise I like to do when I am facing an awkward conversation about money is to imagine that I am having a telepathic conversation with my landlord or boss, for example, ahead of time. It may be useful to imagine that you are speaking to the intended person over the phone or through a live video interaction. Ask for what you need in your imagined meeting and request that it be in the highest good of both parties. Resonate the highest frequency of confidence in yourself in that moment and *believe* in yourself. Know that you are enough. When the actual conversation occurs, remember to be calm and notice how the interaction transforms before your eyes.

As you are elevating your vibrational frequency, remind yourself as often as necessary that you are more powerful than any situation and that worrying is a choice. Imagine how you will feel when you deliver the rent or mortgage payment ahead of the next due date. What would that feel like? How would you act in that reality? Whatever you can imagine, feel and do it now. Hold that feeling and begin to live in harmony with that elevated state of being. Practice this repeatedly until you feel good inside despite any limiting circumstance surrounding you. If in this process, you begin to feel fear, allow that too. Fear in the presence of expansion is a sign that you are testing the boundaries of a prior mindset that you will ultimately leave behind. Learn to use the fear as a gauge of your forward progression. If you do not feel fear, you are not living life big enough. Let the Universe pleasantly surprise you with possibilities. Use these steps to begin walking in the life that you want and love.

Admittedly, given my upbringing and negative beliefs surrounding money, this lesson was one of the most difficult to master. Changing old patterns takes persistence. It is challenging to balance the physical needs of everyday life with energetic internal balance. However, stick to the principles. Releasing the mindset of poverty is far and away the most sustainable way to attract wealth and abundance into your life. The Universe wants to give you what you need and desire, but the universal language of abundance is the feeling of love and confidence, not the feeling of frustration or the chatter of an immature mind. The Universe hears what your heart resonates.

If you have any fear or anger in your heart associated with money, then frightening and anger-provoking situations will show up for you when it comes to financial resources. On the other hand, if your heart resonates with the vibrations of confidence and thankfulness, the Universe has no choice but to give you what you *feel* accordingly.

To effectively resonate high-frequency vibrations and feel genuinely good around money, you must align your thoughts, language, and actions. When money is in your presence, see it, acknowledge it, and offer your gratitude. Be open to cash flow in whichever way it comes that aligns with your purpose. Receiving money should feel as good as giving money. Allow money to flow to and away from you without resistance.

During my journey to overcome the money construct, I became stuck on more than one occasion. Despite doing my conscious, energetic work, I continued to feel contraction surrounding money. I would hear myself thinking that I should be careful not to spend too much money in fear that I would run out of cash. I would find myself in a constricted state holding onto my greenbacks instead of giving freely. I noticed that I would feel moved to donate to a cause only to stop myself because I believed I could not afford it. It was during these moments that I listened to a video seminar on money blocks. The message about tithing resonated deeply within me. Initially, I noticed that I felt negativity when I heard the word tithing. I examined that feeling and recognized that I held dense energy related to a church experience I had in college decades earlier where I was forced to tithe twenty percent of my income. It felt horrible, and anytime I heard the word tithing, I would emotionally contract.

However, I realized through awareness and with the guidance of many who have traveled this path before me, that tithing could look and feel good. I remember I was at a coffee shop when I heard a message about the universal flow of money. At that moment, I looked in my wallet and found $10 in cash. I took ten percent or $1 and tithed to the barista in the form of a tip. I felt great and committed to tithing ten percent of my wealth in any manner I saw fit. In a single moment and with a single act, I felt a lightness within me that opened a fresh, new relationship between me and the flow of money. I realized that I needed to honor the universal law of flow that involves both freely giving and receiving to definitively elevate my vibrational frequency toward plenty.

Take a moment to create a detailed diary of your financial needs and desires. Be as specific as possible in this exercise. Do not worry about how everything will come together. That is the job of the Universe. Instead, focus your attention on the why and what of that which you are creating. Honor yourself as the master creator that you are. Finally, begin to take the forward steps toward your higher frequency goals. As you move forward toward expansion, observe the changes in your feelings toward that of lightness and acceptance. If at any time you feel stuck or sense old patterns returning, acknowledge them using your inner voice. Return to your focused breathing exercises to release the blocks that have been holding you back. Then continue forward again using your affirmations. Repeat this exercise as many times as needed to feel fully in your power regarding money. In this exercise, remember to honor the universal flow of money too in a manner that feels most comfortable for you.

The frequency of abundance is not a belief system. It is an essential truth you must know, learn, and embrace on the ascension path. It helps to align your thinking mind with the high-vibrational resonance of the heart.

Instead of thinking that bills are a burden, see them for what they are. Invoices represent a service you need and the value and money you have agreed to in exchange for that service. Be thankful for receiving the utility, and you will happily pay the bill. Feel great when a bill is paid off. If there is a bill that is still unpaid, imagine how elated you will feel when the debt clears. Attach a high-frequency energy signature to the payment of every obligation for the valued products or services you've received.

If the dwindling balance in your bank account scares you, hold that feeling and ask your higher self the question "Why does this scare me?" What is likely to show up is something much more profound than the idea of bouncing a check. Your fear may be rooted in feelings of inadequacy or shame. Perhaps you have a lingering sense of not being good enough or residual thoughts of being irresponsible with money held within your energetic matrix. No matter what the painful or stifling money belief is for you, allow yourself to feel it. You must first acknowledge any stagnant feelings you are still holding onto regarding money before they can be released.

Reclaim the power you give to money. Verifiable power resides only within you. Forgive yourself and let go. Breathe through your feelings and observe the changes in the energy surrounding your heart. Allow the fear to dissipate entirely. Any time a similar feeling arises again, repeat the process of letting go. You may be clearing dense energy related to money and worth from many lifetimes ago.

Do not be ashamed of carrying emotional baggage related to money and don't hide from it. Facing what is holding you back allows you to move forward. American society doesn't openly speak about personal finances. It is a taboo subject in our culture. Many people do not know the financial status of their spouses, for example. Parents will not always share their financial journeys with their children, and vice versa.

The secrecy around money makes it even more imposing to release limiting emotions because it is socially acceptable to hold everything in, pretending to have it all together. I had to clear numerous money issues before I felt a measurable shift in my forty-sixth year of life. I didn't realize how much negative energy I had to release when it came to money until I traveled out of my body and experienced a money exchange.

During a soul flight, I happened to be in a busy marketplace in what appeared to be a foreign landscape. It felt like I was in a place like Marrakesh, bustling, dusty, and dry. I went to buy something with U.S. dollars from a street vendor who gave me change in a strange currency that reminded me of Monopoly money. Instead of the symbols of the dollar bill, the "fake money" had symbols on it that looked like logos from foreign cigarette companies. As I looked down at the money to count my change, I instantly felt enraged.

I stormed back to the vendor with fighting words at the ready. That merchant duped me, I thought. As I approached, the shopkeeper looked curiously calm, and I would go as far to say amused. I moved to strike her, surprising even myself. I had never behaved this way before. I felt anger boiling inside of me. However, just as suddenly as I went to strike her, I abruptly stopped myself. I had realized this was another test of my energetic frequency. Ethereal wolves weren't chasing me as I had experienced in other dimensions, but I was openly challenged with my concept of money, its power, and my value. I knew I had to release the dense energy attached to me.

Our monetary system is a confusing and highly sophisticated barter system. We exchange goods and services for fancy pieces of paper or metals—or even more abstractly, mere numbers on an electronic interface. The value of money is not more than an agreed-upon consensus. In many of the higher dimensions, there is no use for money as more evolved beings have transcended the money construct entirely. In some less-developed cultures still existing on Earth today, money is not a fluid concept.

The value of a dollar is no more than its consensus value. To a person earning a dollar a day, the dollar is valuable. To another person making a thousand dollars a day, the worth of that same dollar is negligible. The world has collectively designed a monetary system in which we all participate. It is not in our essence to exist in a state of lack. To operate harmoniously within the confines of the system we created, we must work toward energetic balancing.

The money construct is nothing to be feared. It is not unlike the value of any resource the Earth readily provides. We are entitled to it but trust that you are fully supported in this life with or without money. If things do not work out the way you expect, this too is okay. Don't give up on claiming your birthright. The Universe is showing you something about your inner self that you must transmute when money does not show up on time or flow freely to you. You see, financial lack is never about the actual money, it is about an energetic frequency resonating within you.

Most people want more than enough money. Having more than enough satisfies the mind so that it does not worry. Desiring more than enough money is perfectly fine. However, understand that abundance requires a dynamic internal balance. Feeling greedy for wanting more money than you need, for example, is a limiting belief. You must release the underlying feelings associated with greed to have fluid resources. If there are religious beliefs involving feelings of selfishness or guilt, you must transform those beliefs too. Elevating your frequency requires you to reclaim all of your energy.

You cannot vibrate at the energetic frequency of gratitude and abundance if you are still holding on to stifling religious beliefs or restrictive beliefs about yourself. Limiting beliefs cannot hang on for the ride. They must be released. Many of us still live in survival mode, working to pay our bills and survive. We are barely getting by. Throughout life, we look for financial support from others seeking to receive all the money we need with ease. If all the money we needed were merely given to us time after time, we would not be inspired to do the emotional work required to elevate our vibrational frequency. Thereby, we would always need a bailout, and that would not be sustainable. You must expand yourself beyond survival by doing the work of introspection to hold the frequency of abundance.

Expansion of your consciousness and the raising of your frequency regarding money can look like buying quality foods if you have been in the habit of buying the cheapest instead of what is healthiest for you and your family. Tell yourself that you are worth it and that you deserve what is best for you.

Expansion can look like trusting in yourself when you previously have doubted yourself. Trust that your guides, guardians, your higher self, and Source fully support you. If you are living in substandard conditions, there is room for growth to bring up your standard of living. To do so, you must first know that it is possible for you. You must look inside yourself to find the imbalance that has put you in a challenging living situation and do the work of correcting that energetic imbalance. The outer world will transform following the fundamental inner shift because you'll be open to receive more possibilities.

Many people choose their careers based on the pay they expect to earn. In your case, have you placed greater emphasis on collecting a paycheck than doing work aligned with your soul purpose? Expansion can also look like doing a job that contributes to your happiness and fulfillment. You expand when you understand a paycheck is not the primary reason for doing something. When you do purposeful work, wealth and abundance show up because you are performing an undertaking brimming with passion. You will be energized, radiating love and light. It bears pointing out that abundance is not limited to cash alone. If you think lots of money is the definition of wealth, you are in for a pleasant surprise.

Wherever there is room for expansion in your life, bravely leap forward. An emotional breakthrough, like equilibrium, does not happen overnight. Balancing is a process. However, as you move toward equilibrium and expansion, momentum will set in, accelerating the pace of your forward movement in ways you previously would not have thought possible. There is no order of difficulty for the Universe to provide anything at all. Everything is possible as you acclimate to the frequency of love.

As you journey into consciousness, you will understand that financial security is an illusion. Feeling secure in the presence of a growing bank account is false security. Feeling insecure in the face of an empty bank account is a response to false danger and fear. In either situation, you have more faith in the illusion than you have in yourself. Genuine security comes from trusting in yourself in times of greatest uncertainty. It is only the mind that is satisfied with a large bank balance. Large amounts of money give it a break from worrying about the immediate future.

We can be sure of this principle because we know that money cannot buy happiness; it cannot satisfy the soul. Money in the absence of joy becomes worthless and corrupt. What is most important about incarnated life is to have experiences that allow you to feel unconditional love and happiness. Money can facilitate fun experiences and ease the mind's chatter, but life isn't about the accumulation of capital. It is about love.

Like time, the money construct is an illusion of the third dimension. The very survival of the world's financial institutions relies on our continued belief in the construct. Money is not an inherent need for existence. Therefore, it should not possess absolute power. Money is merely a means of exchange. The Earth provides everything needed to survive in great abundance and always has. The monetary system does not exist where human beings do not. Notice that all other life forms on the planet have lived in bountiful numbers over many ages without using any currency. Humans are no different from animals in our ability to stay alive and have fulfilling life experiences in the absence of money.

The truth is that money only solves financial problems which are self-created. It does not heal the soul. The accumulation of capital is not the same as the accumulation of abundance. Money is just one resource on the wealth continuum, whereas abundance encompasses all resources, including happiness, contentment, relationships, and experiences. When you raise your frequency to love prosperously, an ample flow of money will be just one of the many things you attract into your life.

The vibration of abundance resonates from the heart center to bring you excellent health, love, relationships, fulfillment, and joy in all aspects of your life.

CHAPTER 13

Race

In the English language, we define race as a traditional *division* of humankind. An arbitrary classification of modern people based on skin color, eye shape, or facial structure. We have further adapted the definition of race to include the region of an individual's ancestral origin and native language. We choose whatever is convenient to divide and label life energy that is having a human experience. The divisions act as blinders so that we no longer can see what is most important about a person. The arbitrary divisions lend to our forgetting about our oneness—that we are all connected.

But why do we feel the need to divide ourselves? In the most important ways, we are all the same. We are energetic beings who have "descended" to the dense frequency of Earth 3.0 to mature our eternal souls. Before an energy body is assigned a physical existence, it makes an agreement of sorts on the other side of the veil to forget its totality of being and to experience embodied life. If the energy body believed that there was a true difference in the type of physical embodiment it was assuming, why would that soul incarnate as such? Why make life harder than it already is in some cases?

When the life energy enters a body, it does not have an

awareness of its eye shape, skin color, or facial structure. It is just happy to be alive and having a human experience. It takes conditioning of the egoic mind to develop judgmental awareness of the physical self. It is sanctioned conceit that exalts one physical attribute while disparaging another. Thinking that one person is better than another person is a deception that gives credence to the race construct. Racial divisions exist only in the densest of minds.

Cultural conditioning plays a role in the dividing of humankind on the planet and is the basis for some racial labels. Culture and ethnicity are not good or bad, and one is not better than another. Societal values are often carried down from past generations and are highly dependent on the region of the world and the civilization someone happens to be born into. It is the belief that one national ethos is superior to another that creates harm for those with differing ideas. It is the intolerance of one nation or the dominance of another that disturbs the balance. All that is in existence is allowed. However, it is not for one culture to destroy another no matter who thinks they are better.

It is true that cultures are in different phases along the evolutionary path. If you look at the past, you will see that every advanced culture today was once very dense in ideology, vibrating energetically at a stiflingly low frequency. Just as individual people are in different places on their life paths, so too are individual cultures and the countries that groups of similar people inhabit. Just as you may not be able to have relationships with all people, nations may not have the ability to communicate or fully understand one another during a given age.

National relationships, just like interpersonal relationships, change over the multitude of moments making up their existence.

Governments of the world representing large cultural bodies reflect the vibrational frequencies and imbalances of their constituents. If you have ever thought, *How could they elect such a president?* you'll need to look no further than a nation's people. The government is a mirror of a highly resonant frequency in the country. It may not be *your* frequency, but it is very much there in the minds and thoughts of a great many citizens. The mirror may reflect what you do not want to see around you, but the existence of the resonating frequency must be acknowledged and worked though. It is not unlike a problem or fear that you have kept deep inside because you are afraid of feeling or acknowledging it. Like the personal issue you are avoiding, the prevailing vibration of a society will have no choice but to declare itself and rise. Only in this way can the energy finally be released, allowing the collective group to move forward.

Every nation has work to do to elevate its frequency. Every group of people has within it differing thoughts and philosophies that are looking for some way to balance themselves for the good of the whole. When there are mass migrations of people from one nation to another in times of war or due to natural shifts in climate or other environmental considerations, an imbalance occurs. This imbalance of energy is felt when the thoughts and ideologies of one group overwhelm another.

Know that every being is trying to evolve while embodied, to achieve some cosmic equilibrium. It is what we all have in common.

As members of the human species, when we label and divide things we also attach emotions and feelings to them. We sort any number of things into contrasting categories, like clean or dirty, good or bad, high or low, and in or out. In the same manner that we sort dirty laundry, we sort and compartmentalize people, cultures, and countries. We also internalize the rhetoric of individuals who have forgotten their true nature to justify the divisions between us, thereby empowering dense thinking.

The concept of race is elementary and has no consistent basis. It is yet another human construct, this one having no real value or true meaning. It comes from forgetting our higher selves and having amnesia about our past. I sometimes wonder why we can accept all animal species as they are but not the human species in its entirety. Animals are revered as a source of wonder and are protected for the betterment of life on Earth. Some animals or insects exist to the detriment of humans, biting or stinging us, spreading disease, or causing death to our physical bodies. Yet, we see the value of allowing all creatures to exist. We recognize that every living being on the Earth has a place in the ecosystem and that a loss of a species is of detriment to the whole. The diversity of the animal kingdom is both accepted and respected. However, we cannot manage do the same for the diversity of human life.

Is a polar bear more magnificent than a panda bear? Is a chocolate Labrador somehow inferior to a yellow Labrador? Why do we respect the splendid diversity of animal species only to marginalize diverse groups within our own species? Why must we cling to silly excuses to demote the life experience of one being while exalting another simply for its physical appearance?

There is utility in identifying genetic groups of people that help the medical community define and treat debilitating conditions that typically occur in a specific genotype. It is important to recognize, however, that every person in a culture, even those sharing a common language or looking alike, may not share the same genotypic expression. Medical diagnosis is not a reason to racially divide all of humanity. It is not right to judge people negatively by the way they look on the outside. If you make an effort to know a person, you will inevitably find that you have more in common than not. What tends to create the most extreme differences are the frequencies associated with cultural norms and the evolutionary distance a person has progressed along his or her life path.

Racial qualification is an attempt to further label and separate energy beings having a human experience. A prodigious absurdity is attached to racial and ethnic labels that implies a judgment on a group. You do not have to agree with another group or embrace their culture, but we must accept that they rightfully exist. You can be thankful if you have advanced along your evolutionary path and no longer hold on to the dense thought forms of racial prejudice. You are simply learning something else in this lifetime. If you feel the need to distance yourself from certain individuals, countries, or cultures, do so understanding that you are not better, but are just in a different vibrational place than those energy beings. You can now see the struggle inherent in the lessons another group of beings is tasked with learning.

Some racial labels extend to include religious beliefs of various groups. Popular beliefs about the Jewish culture extending from World War II, for example, are blatantly untrue.

All Polynesians are not one thing. All Chinese are not one thing. All Africans are not one thing. All Latinos are not one thing. All Europeans are not one thing. Your true self has a frequency that's all its own even if you were raised by a family of knuckleheads. Frequency is an individual soul resonance.

Other racial contexts involve skin color. White and black, for example, have greater utility in an artist's palette than when describing a person. Using color to qualify race is of no worth and fails to define any human being. Nobody's skin is either black or white. Black and white are two colors in the visual light spectrum. What sets them apart is their different frequencies. Humans have skin qualities based on their geographic region of origin. These qualities are encoded on everyone's DNA. Furthermore, all human beings vibrate at a much lower frequency than any color on the visible light spectrum.

The skin is the largest organ of the physical body that helps the embodied being adapt to its native surroundings. Skin is the outer shell of a person and says nothing of real importance about the true being carrying the body. A color or pigment cannot define character, beliefs, ideas, aptitude, or consciousness. The skin is a physical body part just like the spleen and liver are body parts. What is the point of dividing humans based on common and necessary bodily organs?

We all have skin and need skin to exist on the planet. Of what use is such a division? The body is only a shell, housing the spirit while on Earth. What is most important about any human being is invisible to the eye.

Another absurdity of the race construct is that it implies that groups of people speaking the same language or those born in the same country also have shared beliefs and character traits. The concept of race is a fallacy because it does not recognize the individual and fails to acknowledge that what is most important about any person remains unseen. There are millions upon millions of people speaking a common language. Does language help us to qualify disease processes? Does common language inform us of culture or belief systems? Does native language inform us about the constitution of a character or the soul of a being?

Not all racial divisions are rooted in racism. When racism occurs, however, it is of the lowest and densest energy embodied by humanity. Racism is rooted in hate, which is the lowest of all energetic frequencies. Racism is entrenched in fear and insecurity. You need only to look at the facial expressions and body language of those who are expressing hatred. There is a visceral fear and insecurity of that hating soul's true value and a near-complete separation of that physical being from its higher self. The being's dual nature is unknown to it.

We feel hate when we are disconnected from Source energy—from God, if that term resonates more with you. Hating another being for no reason is ultimately hating yourself, as we are all connected to Source. If you have ever looked at another individual and had an immediate feeling of dislike, you were simply seeing a mirror, reflecting you to yourself. Ask yourself what is honestly bothering you about the existence of another human being. You will find on introspection that the problem isn't with the other being. The discord lies within you.

When you have an automatic fear or prejudice about another, it is a sign that there is a dense energy inside of you that has attached itself to your heart. There is a belief system that is no longer serving you that must be released.

Releasing a dense energy that provokes hate in you can be accomplished by suspending judgment for a moment and communicating with the other person. Say hello, good morning, or good evening. When you offer a simple act of kindness that acknowledges and shows respect for another living being, the hate begins to transform immediately. As with transmuting any feeling, you must align your thoughts and actions with the higher-vibration feeling.

If previously you thought that someone who looked a certain way could not be trusted, for example, transmute this belief with a kind greeting and address the negative thought by telling yourself something like, *Hmm, maybe I was wrong about this person.* It might also help to imagine that if another being took one look at you and had the same judgment, how would that make you feel? The idea is not to be best friends with everyone you encounter. The goal is to release negative, dense energy so that when your time comes, you can transcend the third dimension.

Use your own words, thoughts, and feelings to challenge your long-held beliefs about race, nationality, and ethnicity. Repeating the exercise every time you begin to feel a hateful feeling emerging will go a long way in releasing dense energy that has attached itself to you, dimming your divine light.

CHAPTER 14

Religion

My first memories of religion date back to the late 1970s, attending my paternal grandmother's Baptist church. I recall the hustle on Sunday mornings to ready ourselves to hear the word of God. I would wear my best dress and shoes and parade around like it was the most special of days. My early childhood experiences were in Sunday school, singing songs like "Yes, Jesus Loves Me," coloring religious pictures, eating candy, and having a potluck supper in the church basement. Sunday supper was always fried chicken, green beans, macaroni and cheese, and some flavor of sweet punch. Dessert would be a homemade cake or banana pudding with bananas and cookie wafers. I also remember becoming old enough to go upstairs to sit in the sanctuary as a child. I found it rather boring but remember the pastor having an intangible quality that drew people to him. When we were upstairs, I saw that the gang of grandchildren in our family only stressed my grandmother, who was ever busy with her lady friends, keeping up appearances. One of my cousins would pick gum off the bottom of the pew and rechew it. Another cousin would drool down his arm, waving it in the air as if Christ himself was bleeding from his palms. I was amused and appalled at the same time while beholding our actions. I imagined our untamed nature made us look like a bunch of hooligans.

On one extraordinary Sunday, I was to be baptized, along with my brothers and a few cousins. I suspect my grandmother must have arranged the spectacle in an effort to save our souls. I remembered seeing adults baptized in the church on past occasions, but I hadn't seen kids baptized before. My mind told me that this wasn't an ordinary occasion but an all-important one. There was a different kind of energy in the chapel on baptism day. It wasn't the usual old ladies in fancy hats fainting or waving their hands high in the air and saying words like, "Thank you, Jesus" and "Praise the Lord." My cousins and I thought such scenes were particularly funny and we would giggle and mimic the fainting ladies. On baptism day, there was an unmistakable reverence in the air, a kind of witnessing of hope. An anticipation of something better to come.

Although I knew it was a very special day, I had no idea what it meant to be baptized. It just looked like being dunked under the water. Deep inside, I felt terrified.

I thought it strange that I was getting baptized in my nightgown and footie socks. All the grandkids were dressed in our pajamas. There were six of us in total, not one over the age of six years. The pastor gave his big sermon. I don't recall a single word of it. Then it was time to be baptized. We all stood up and walked single file toward a mysterious door that led us behind the pulpit. Being baptized was an experience out of the ordinary. On that day, we all were on our best behavior. I wasn't the first to go, so I stood in line and waited my turn. I remember thinking how brave everyone was. No one voiced any concerns. The pastor would say a blessing and dunk the kid whose turn it was under the water.

When it was my turn, I walked up three or four stairs and found myself at the edge of a large rectangular pit filled with water. It was dark water and I could not see to the bottom. There was a large mirror over the pit that allowed the congregation to see what was happening during the baptism. I noticed the pastor standing in the middle of the pool, fully dressed from head to toe in a suit and a big, colorful velvet robe. The water was deep, covering his waist. He extended his hand to help me down a couple of steps into the water. The water was warm to my surprise and soft. It moved gently. When I was completely down, I walked a few steps on my tiptoes toward the pastor, the water covering my chest. The reverend lifted me onto his feet and I noticed that he was wearing his leather shoes. Just like those that had come before me, he said his prayer for my soul and then whispered to me, "Hold your breath."

When it was over, the six of us were paraded, dripping wet, in front of the congregation. I can only imagine what that must have looked like. I am so grateful that Instagram was not invented in the 1970s. I don't remember feeling any different after my dunking, just wet and exposed. But I was now baptized according to an old Southern tradition, I believe. I guess that was when I officially became a Christian.

Soon after the baptism, my father remarried and moved our family just over the border from Pennsylvania to West Virginia. That is where I started the first grade. Despite his upbringing and the religiosity of his mother, my father was not a religious man. For the remainder of my childhood, I rarely went to church—only on holidays or when we visited my grandmother. I didn't know it at the time, but my father saw something that disturbed him deeply in that church where I was baptized. Something happened there that turned him away from the church forever. I spoke to him about it when I was all grown up. I still only know that he saw something; he has never shared with me exactly what that something was.

Despite my father's lack of association with the church, I was very interested in God while I was growing up. I was a believer. At sixteen, I started going to church on my own and thought I might want to join a convent. I was not Catholic, yet I knew that I wanted to be of service to humanity and for a moment believed that religious servitude was the most honorable of vocations. This was the age at which I first began to articulate the desire to know my purpose. I began to wonder why I was here and sought to do what was my purpose. This seeking led me to be heavily involved in various church groups and organizations.

I was conscientious of my choices, fearing that God was not only watching my every move but also judging me. I feared that I would not go to heaven if I did too many things wrong. I set out on a journey of little perfections. Everything I did I wanted to be perfect in the eyes of God. I imagined that I would graduate college, get married, and have my first child by age twenty-six. I would then have the time to bear two more children approximately two years apart before thirty. I thought I should be the dutiful homemaker with perfect kids and a perfect little life. I also wanted the perfect career to match.

Well, none of that happened for me. Nor could a perfectly idealized existence happen for anyone because we all descend to Earth to learn something new. In my case, I began to question the very institution of religion and its expectations on me during college, after I joined a progressive church that wanted to control every aspect of my life. This church wanted to dictate how I dressed, where I went on vacation, and even where I attended medical school. This group seemed more concerned with my income and tithing twenty percent of it than about my wellbeing. Attending that church was the first time I experienced fear associated with religion.

I fled that organization and went away to medical school only to quickly join a Christian medical group. I found myself further disillusioned by talk that I was somehow chosen and special because I believed in the Christian way to connect with God. I doubted this notion and could not imagine that if I were born in another country and believed in the religion of that land, I would somehow be less in the eyes of an omnipotent God.

I remember living abroad for the calendar year 1994 in Ghana, West Africa. It was my final year of college. I was an exchange student for the first six months on the campus of the University of Ghana at Legon. My final six months were spent in small villages, working in rural health clinics. Before I lived abroad, I thought myself poor. I lived in a marginal apartment paying $200 a month in rent that I earned waitressing at a restaurant. I had an old car that I purchased replacement parts for directly from a junkyard. When I would drive this car, it never failed that the radiator would smoke when I was idling at a stoplight. I would drive away embarrassed and as quickly as possible to dissipate the smoke.

I was living the life of the average, struggling American college student. This is when I still appreciated a good meal at home with my parents.

When I was working at the health clinics in Ghana, I saw real poverty. Poverty of person, of place, and of the mind. It was the first time I saw children with polio, a disease that had long been eradicated in the United States. I saw a child with an elephantiasis limb so swollen that it sent me to sleep with sad nightmares and lingering memories. I was working in a health clinic one afternoon when a father rushed through the door with a little child of no more than seven years. The father was speaking his native tongue, that which was unintelligible to me, but I understood his unrest as he presented his child. The boy was lethargic but standing. He began vomiting what looked like bright red, fluffy billows of diseased matter. The lightness of the matter that landed on the dirt floor of the clinic told me this was not from the stomach but from the lung. The child died of tuberculosis on the dirt floor of that modest bush clinic mere moments later. There was nothing that could be done.

I thought long and hard about this boy and his tragic death. I looked around me, at the clinic and the staff, at the village, at the country, and then I imagined the continent. I pondered the whole of the world. This world, I thought, could not be related to the God I worshipped. *Perhaps there is no God at all,* I thought.

I would return to the United States with unanswered questions about all of religion. I did not completely lose faith, but my ground was indeed shaken. I asked many friends about their religious beliefs and institutions and found that most people's lives and beliefs were rife with hypocrisy. I would meet self-proclaimed devout Catholics who did not *believe* in birth control but would engage in premarital sex and then have abortions if they got knocked up. I would hear about corruption throughout in the ranks of the Catholic Church with heinous tales of secrecy and debauchery. The Catholic way to God, I decided, was also one I could not follow.

I went on to medical school soon after and continued seeking the truth about life and answers to my questions about the human condition. By this time in my life, I was in my mid-twenties. I wondered if Christianity was not the answer. Maybe an eastern philosophy, like Buddhism, would have the answers I sought. I studied the path of Siddhartha Gautama after graduation from medical school and tried chanting and meditating. Studying the Buddha's path, however, did not bring me any closer to my truth. I found the people practicing the Buddhist ideology to have lives as messy and complicated as mine. And I came to understand that enlightenment does not require the complete sacrifice of the physical body to achieve. Nevertheless, no one seemed to have the answer to their purpose and reason for being.

For more than a decade that followed, I had no religion at all. I didn't affiliate with any institutional faith. I felt alone at times and avoided talking about religion. Being a nonbeliever was somehow too scary a position for many people to tolerate it. Then I began reading about existentialism and the philosophies of Albert Einstein, Friedrich Nietzsche, and Faulkner. I would read books written by people who identified themselves as agnostics or atheist. Everyone seemed to be searching for the eternal truth about their existence. In this pursuit, I was not alone.

The answers about who I am and my purpose ultimately came from looking inward, toward my true self. Only in this introspective pursuit did I find the answers I was seeking. It is true, I am here to give service to humanity. It is only now that I know how I am going to do it and why.

Religion, I have found, has a purpose. In its purest form, it provides an ideology for how to lead our lives on Earth in harmony with all of nature and every other living being. The foundation of all the major faiths asks us to love our neighbor and to treat others as we would like to be treated. At the unadulterated root of religion is love.

Religions become corrupt when the words or scriptures are manipulated to oppress any single group or individual. And when the truth about the divine light within every human being is hidden in a shroud of secrecy.

Each being is divine in spirit and has descended to Earth for a divine purpose. We all are encoded with a rightful path. Because we have free will, we often embark upon our chosen paths. We pursue our chosen paths because we think it is what we are supposed to do. This comes from limiting belief systems and a lack of trust in the order of the Universe.

Sometimes our chosen paths are dictated by others who have not yet fulfilled their own personal desires. When a chosen path is not congruent with the rightful path, it cannot be sustained. It drains us so that we travel on the chosen path until we can no longer stand it. Then a place for change and growth is created for us by the Universe. In the most misaligned instances, we take an outright wrongful path, leaving the scars of pain and destruction in our wake.

Religion is a human construct that has been changed and altered over the millennia. Many Christians today are taught using the King James version of the Holy Bible without giving it a second thought. In my experience, few have questioned why this is or have asked what King James' motives were for printing a new version of a sacred text. How many of us, regardless of our faiths, are taught about the burning of the Ancient Library of Alexandria in Egypt in the third century before the Common Era? It is estimated that nearly 400,000 ancient scrolls were lost, symbolizing the greatest loss of human cultural knowledge in Earth's long history. It is no wonder that we have lost our way.

Religion is something created and retrofitted by humankind for use in the physical world. It has been adapted and reinterpreted in many instances to capture the changing of tides and motivations of religious leaders. Religions as we have designed them, do not have applicability outside of the 3D Earth structure.

Enlightenment doesn't require tithing, brainwashing, submitting to any rituals, or genuflection. Enlightenment does not require special clothing, rote memorization of texts, or worship of any person, living or dead. Spiritual beings who have come before you can serve as your guides, but you must remember that they too lead imperfect lives and had to engage in the work of introspection to achieve their awakenings. Don't put your teachers up on a pedestal—not even if they have OBEs.

If you must believe in something, first believe in yourself. Your higher self is not something to believe in, it is your life force and an aspect of you that you will want to know intimately. The higher self that I refer to again and again is the whole of you, your true self existing beyond the physical as well as within the physical body. This is the infinite expression of the divine you.

Enlightenment is not an impossible pursuit, it is a manner of being. It is for anyone who does the work of introspection to ascend higher and higher into expanded consciousness.

PART THREE

Perspective on Life after Multidimensional Travel

Beyond the experience of leaving the body and exploring other dimensions, multidimensional travel brings with it core tenants of learning and ancient remembering. Waking up to conscious awareness provides new perspectives on just about every aspect of life. We have numerous hang-ups as individuals and as a collective society. In Part Three, I will share some perspectives about life on Earth that I have gained over the past several years on my path of ascending consciousness. These perspectives are more personal than the descriptions of the human constructs in Part Two, which were also gained from my experiences of out-of-body, multidimensional travel.

Higher-frequency consciousness allows us to tap into the higher realms for renewed understanding of a variety of topics. As you follow your path to higher awareness, you will begin to access wisdom that transcends time and space, going far beyond everything you have learned in the physical world. There is simplicity in the great complexity unfolding life. Honest dialogue with my higher self and the spiritual entities known by many on Earth as the ascended masters informs my newfound perspectives on our shared human existence.

Incremental

Within the immeasurable Universe,
There is the measure of you.
Each day you decide.
What you decide,
Slowly, incrementally, inexorably
Becomes the reality of you.
Are you incrementally false?
Or are you incrementally true?

—JOHN DALTON

CHAPTER 15

Authenticity

In life, it's easy to spend an inordinate amount of time trying to be somebody we are not. It starts very early on as we try to please our parents or to imitate older siblings and other children. As we grow, we seek ways to fit in, to be accepted by peers. We try on different clothing styles and manners of being to look cool, or smart, or even rebellious. Some of this is experimentation, a normal aspect of human development. Even so, there's a pull to fit in. The inauthenticity continues into early adulthood as we try to emulate whatever we think it means to be accomplished or acceptable. We try different sports or hobbies. We even try on new attitudes to see what sticks. There is a perpetual looking outward to figure out who we really are.

The irony in all of this is that on the inside we are who we've always been. Oftentimes, we may feel afraid to openly display our true selves for fear of rejection. What we fail to understand very early on is that there is a good chance that the real you is spectacularly different than everyone you've ever met.

Inauthenticity is not trying new things on the path of self-discovery. Inauthenticity is persisting in trying to be someone or something you are not. Inauthenticity doesn't feel right. It will likely feel burdensome and require a lot of effort. You will likely feel some form of internal resistance or awkwardness. An inauthentic action might be something you do to show that you are good enough. Many forms of inauthenticity are attempts at self-validation.

I was visiting the South of France over the New Year holiday in 2017. I was staying at a lovely hotel in Nice overlooking the Mediterranean Sea. As I looked out toward the horizon to admire the incredible view, I noticed a great many pedestrians walking along la Promenade des Anglais. The weather was a comfortable, sunny 60 degrees Fahrenheit (16 degrees Celsius). The scene on the Promenade appeared calm and routine with a mix of old and young people appreciating the day. What stood out to me as unusual was the number of individuals wearing fur coats. Some of the coats were short, and others were full length, almost touching the ground. I would again observe this ostentatious display while visiting Monaco during this same holiday.

My reaction? I thought to myself, *How can anyone tolerate wearing a full-length fur coat in sunny, 60-degree weather?* On further inspection, I found the people wearing the coats to be full of insecurities. It wasn't enough to be themselves to feel they fit in. These posers had to show onlookers their financial status by modeling the fur coats they wore. The charade was as absurd as it was inauthentic. The wearers of the coats did not look any happier or richer than the persons not wearing fur, just more ridiculous.

I ask you, if you feel that you must parade your proxies for wealth in front of strangers to prove something, are you truly wealthy?

As phony as the pretense on the Promenade was, I was not in the position to judge. I had to remember my own longstanding inauthenticity. It dealt with my hair.

For most of my life, I tried to make my curly hair straight. It sounds silly, but I did this for thirty-two years. It started when I was a child. My mother or aunt would straighten my hair, so it would be easier to manage and look "acceptable." I bought in to the idea that this was important to do, and when I became old enough, I used chemicals and heat to straighten my hair myself. Ultimately, it got to the point where I no longer felt comfortable being myself. I didn't have the self-confidence to be seen in public without straightened hair. I had been told (and believed) that I could not get a job if my hair wasn't straight. My flimsy self-esteem was built upon maintaining the illusion of being someone I was not.

Keeping curly hair straight is not "easier" at all. It took me incredible effort to maintain my hair and the chemicals were harmful to my body. I would have to chemically straighten my hair every six weeks and use heat every day to keep up the image. Over the years, the unhealthy illusion became the new normal. No matter what I did, my hair would try to revert to its natural texture, causing me angst.

At the moment of my conscious awakening, I decided that I no longer wished to be somebody I am not. The first thing to go was all the time, money, and energy I had spent worrying about having straight hair. I began to finally let go of the burden of being someone I am not. It felt so good to finally be free of the inauthenticity. I hated worrying about my hair all the time. So long as I was concerned about my hair, I could not happy. It was all such a waste of time and energy. Now I believe that if I had spent the previous thirty-two years learning to accept myself—not only my hair, but everything that's true about me—my life would have been so much easier to manage. It is hard work keeping up a false image. And it frankly serves no one. It involves hiding and lying and there is always a risk of being discovered.

Some forms of inauthenticity come at great cost. It is for each person to decide if it is worth it to maintain their disingenuousness.

Long before I made the decision to wear my hair in its natural state, I had given up wearing makeup and uncomfortable clothes and shoes. In western society, women are encouraged, or even mandated, to wear high-heeled shoes to look professional and polished. Every woman who has tried to live up to this standard knows how painfully uncomfortable those shoes can be.

Like many women in their twenties, I was dressed in heels to attend a party with a good friend one weekend. As I stood outside before entering, I looked down at my feet and wondered, *Why am I doing this to myself?* My feet would ache and sometimes swell from the unnatural pressure I was putting on them. I realized then that the men I could potentially meet at this party or any other event were not worth harming my feet.

When I was even younger and unaware, I would curse my feet for not fitting well into certain shoes. I would become angry at them when they would swell and become injured rather than blame the shoes for being uncomfortable. A major shift occurred within me during my awakening period. I threw out all my high heels and found comfortable work and dress heels of no more than an inch and a half in height.

I chose comfort over trying to impress anyone. What did I have to prove anyway? Once I was awake, it made no sense to me at all to try.

The beauty of waking up was how I began to honor not only my feet, but my entire body for carrying me through my life. I apologized to my feet for abusing them for so many years. If I hurt myself in any way, I began apologizing to myself and promised to be more careful going forward. I noticed immediately that my body responded in kind.

Before waking up consciously, I never thought about my body as its own entity, something that was both connected and separate from me. My body had endured much pain during its life. Conscious awareness helped me to appreciate it.

There is no single thing that you should do or wear to impress others. The only imperative is to be yourself. Your inauthenticity may be in how you present your financial status to the world, your manner of being, remaining in a marriage devoid of love, or hiding under wigs when you have no hair at all. It doesn't matter what your mimicry is. Whatever it is, let it go. When you allow your true self to shine through your actions and appearance, you can begin to offer your distinctive gifts to the world.

Part of the reason we go about leading inauthentic lives is so that we are accepted by others. Inauthenticity is far reaching. It can involve sexual orientation, gender assignment, belief systems, or any manner of pretending. It is understandable that we would try different things as we evolve in this life, but the goal of experimentation should be to decide what is best aligned with the *real* you. You cannot know if you like chocolate ice cream until you try it. But saying you like chocolate when you don't is inauthentic. It is not inauthentic to try new things. Inauthenticity is to persist in being someone you are not.

Be yourself. Have your own thoughts, opinions, and ideas. Embrace your own style. Have unique and fulfilling experiences. Live your life to its fullest. Be authentic. A quote often credited to Oscar Wilde may say this best: "Be yourself. Everyone else is already taken."[1]

CHAPTER 16

Relationships

Our interactions with other embodied beings are *relationships*, whether the relationships are casual acquaintanceships, work relationships, friendships, marriages, or familial relationships. Perhaps the most important and neglected of all the relationships any of us have are the ones we have with ourselves. We relate to each other in many ways and each relationship scenario has expectations attached to it. Some of the deepest pain we feel in life is a result of how we perceive and behave in the relationships we are in.

The relationship you have with yourself is an interesting one, in that it is rooted in the duality of your being. However, it is important to acknowledge your body as an entity in its own right. You must relate to it as well as your spirit. The body is the physical you that carries you through all manner of situations while you're on the planet, so you want to protect it from injury and denigration.

The physical body is often abused with overwork, and with poisons like cigarette smoke and alcohol. Our bodies endure further mishandling from chemicals in the food, water, and air we breathe. We further harm the body with medications, and recreational drugs. We are often displeased with the appearance of the body and attempt to alter it with cosmetics, wigs, tattoos, piercings, and surgeries. We often overfeed the body while at the same time deprive the body of what it really needs to function best: clean foods, pure water, and balanced nutrition.

How many times have you apologized for harming your body or thanked your body for carrying you the distance or even asked your body what it needs? Your body is a living, breathing, complex organism, and each of its cells has its own energy and consciousness. If you are like the rest of us, you likely spend an inordinate amount of time caring for other people's bodies and asking what they need. Try asking and doing for your own body instead.

If you really take the time and effort to listen to your body, you will begin to hear and understand what it really wants. If you are willing to listen to your body, you will hear what it requires to maintain a healthy weight, clear skin, a youthful appearance, and generalized well-being.

The relationship you have with yourself goes beyond the physical. Your energy body has needs too. These needs are largely emotional. The primary needs of the energy body are the needs to be acknowledged and heard. Ignorance of your nonphysical self leads to a perpetual lack of acknowledgment of your true self. The energy body is also your connection to Source energy and the root of your consciousness; as such, it wants to guide you.

To begin to hear the voice of your true self, you must be comfortable being alone with yourself. Most people do not like themselves very much, so they can't stand to be alone. Many can't tolerate being quiet long enough to hear their true selves speak; and if they could, they would not listen to them anyway. You need to cultivate this ability.

Being alone is not the same as being lonely. As you begin to get better acquainted with yourself, you will likely find that you have a lot of catching up to do. If you don't already, you will begin to enjoy the time you have with yourself.

When you are comfortable with yourself, you will no longer need to distract yourself from your thoughts or feelings with music, television, or mindless conversation. You will be okay just being quiet sometimes. Quiet alone time like this gives you the opportunity to learn your purpose and get back on your rightful path. If your relationship with yourself is not the best and most trusted relationship you have, then there's work to be done.

Romantic love relationships are also very important. It does not matter who you love, but that you take the opportunity to experience the profoundness of true romantic love in your lifetime. Romantic love relationships can be tricky because we secretly hope our feelings for our significant other will remain unchanged. In life, there is nothing more constant than change itself. No situation has permanence. Just as we change as individuals, romantic relationships also change over time.

Think of your relationship with your child or parent. The expectation is that the relationship will evolve as both the child and the parents mature. We expect parent-child relationships to change so we don't resist changes or regret them once a change has occurred. We may think back wistfully on a child's infancy or have fond memories of our aging parents from when they were young and strong, but we accept the way life has affected them. It is a natural evolution that is both necessary and beneficial. Or in the case of an older adult—inevitable.

However, we let go of the infant and child we raised and

accept that the adult has emerged. Perhaps we do not fully embrace the adult being, but we accept that the child has become an adult with different needs, views, and ideas about life. We welcome and expect a different relationship with our twenty-five-year-old child than we had with the child at five years of age.

We tend not to have the same expectation in romantic relationships. We somehow expect them to be static as if the partners involved cease to grow emotionally and interpersonally. We want to retain the feelings we had when we first fell in love. Retention is an unrealistic expectation, given that we don't stop maturing at eighteen when we are qualified as adults by society. The process of interpersonal growth spans a lifetime. A person who is a "perfect" partner for you in your twenties could be the antithesis of the person you need in your life at age forty.

Some may find partners early in life who mature at similar rates and in similar directions. However, many couples stay together for religious reasons, financial reasons, feelings of guilt or obligation, children, fear of being alone, the belief of failure, or cultural shame. When staying together for such reasons is not the case, it is a reasonable assumption that connected individuals grow apart emotionally *and* physically. Because we engage in the legal act of marriage, the reality of growing apart gives us pause. It is often not the person we resist letting go of, it is the assets, routines, or status quo that we do not want to part with. We forget that marriage is only a legal contract and in no way determines how we feel emotionally, or more importantly, what we need at a particular point in our lives.

Although marriage can be associated with an emotional connection, it does not necessarily mean the feeling between spouses is love or that love will outlast the marriage. Even in instances of true love, the meaning and the feelings associated with that loving bond will change and evolve over time. The meaning of marriage is culturally subjective, just as the customs and ceremonies to declare marriage to a community are culturally bound. The true measure of a love relationship is the love and respect you have for one other, not whether you qualify to file a joint tax return or jointly own property.

Growing apart emotionally is not a failure. It is the actions that occur as a result of the disconnection that are regrettable. Like many behaviors that are poorly displayed by adults, the behavior many people exhibit while divorcing someone likely tops the list. Divorce or separation is not necessarily the failure of a single individual. Sometimes separation is simply necessary as people move forward on their path of emotional or spiritual maturity. Contrary to consensus, a separation can be a timely opening. Although that may sound counterintuitive due to the feuding over assets, letting go of a past relationship can be liberating. If one person in a relationship is growing apart from the other, then the second partner usually can feel what is happening, even if they are afraid and do not admit it.

It can be uncomfortable to establish a new routine or to break from a habitual behavior in a past relationship. When the ties are finally broken, both people can emerge anew, poised to take the next steps in their life journeys. It is important to remember that if the people involved in a relationship are not perfect, the relationship itself will not be perfect. Thereby, no relationship on Earth is perfect.

Different people are appropriate at different times in your life. Do not beat yourself up if it turns out that the mother or father of your child(ren) is not your lifetime partner. Just as your child matures away from you, so may your partner. The interpersonal growth in no way absolves either parent from the responsibility of raising the child or respecting the other. You may just be doing the job of childrearing in two different locations. In the process, you will discover how different your needs are from those of your child's other parent. Having differences does not give you license to disparage the other parent. Accept that you have differences and now have the space to grow independently. Don't be ashamed of your choices. They likely fulfilled a need you had in the past.

Relationships tend to be rich in lessons. The major fault arising from a broken relationship would be not learning something from the experiences you had with another sentient being.

Early in my awakening, when I had my first Reiki session, I wept tears that came from a place deep inside me and knew what I had to do: I had to separate from my spouse, the father of my son, and start anew. It took me another two years after knowing what I had to do for me to actually do it. I was afraid to leave him because I could not know what the future would hold. I was afraid to go forward on my own with a toddler in tow. I also was uncertain about my financial future and how I could support myself and my child. Furthermore, I was unsure how dual parenting would work out between us as I had only witnessed disastrous separations among family and friends.

The moment came to me in the middle of the night. I awoke to find the other side of the bed empty. It was around three o'clock in the morning in early December 2014. It was my habit to do a relationship "reality check" every year on the anniversary of our decision to lead our lives together. It had occurred on July first for the previous seven years. On that day, I would simply ask my spouse if he still wanted to go through life together with me. And he'd ask me the same question. Did we want to give it another year? Up until this point, the answer we both gave was a resounding "yes" and we went about our usual day. Though we never married, we had a relationship that spanned fifteen years and we had lived together for seven and a half of those years. We had one child together who had turned five years old two months earlier.

While my partner was aware of my out-of-body experiences, I don't think he was aware of the changes occurring inside me as a result. When I awoke in the middle of the night in early December, I knew he was alone in the basement two levels down, watching television. This in itself, did not bother me. It had become normal. Feeling too tired to get out of bed, I texted him my usual reality check question: "Do you think we should continue living together?" He did not text me back. Instead, he raced upstairs to my bedside and asked me what was going on. I said I just felt that I had to do another reality check. I needed to know that we were still on the same page.

It turned out that we were. A couple of days later, we had a very long talk. A talk we should have had ages prior. We both aired our grievances and ultimately decided that we wanted to give walking through life alone a try. There was no drama, just understanding. We did not suddenly hate one another, and we chose not to disparage each other. We agreed to demonstrate a united front as parents and that we would not say negative things about one another to our child. We did not fight. Nothing got broken. I did not want any assets or child support from him. In that moment, I trusted that I would be able to support myself and my son. Between the two of us, we decided to share custody equally and decided I would inform our son about the separation.

Separations can be full of drama, but they don't have to be. At the end of the day, my former partner told me how brave I was even to have broached the topic with him. He admitted that he would have just kept going on, maintaining the status quo if I had not. It turned out that I had freed us both from a future together rife with unfulfillment. I was changing, and he felt it. It was no secret; we just didn't know how to talk about it.

When I woke up in the middle of the night with my reality check, I did not have a plan. But sure enough, one unfolded piece by piece in a manner only the Universe could bring about. Just over a week later, I took my son apartment hunting with me. I told him I was going to live in an apartment and that he would have his own special room there. At the time, my son did not question me much about this. I decided to live within a mile and a half of our existing family residence to ease the transition. That way we all kept our same routines and support systems in place. I secured a place just after Christmas and moved into it on January 15, 2015.

The separation was hard on my son, no doubt about it. I think he cried at bedtime just about every night for the first year on days that he was alone with his father. Prior to the separation, I was his primary caretaker and not having me in the house disturbed him deeply. Naturally, I felt about an inch tall, just awful. My son asked me why I moved away from Daddy's house to live in an apartment. I told him I was looking for happiness. He aptly reminded me saying "Mommy, you can't find happiness in an apartment."

Of course, I understood that. What I needed was the space

to find my internal happiness. I was looking for inner quiet, a way to be actualized.

Higher consciousness was changing me and my relationships. This was a major shift—perhaps the greatest single shift of a relationship in my entire life. I realized that all my relationships had been steadily changing throughout my life. This romantic one was just more significant because there was now a child involved. Even though I would no longer live with his father, I still had to have some type of relationship with him. My prior *modus operandi* would have been to literally run away and never speak to him again. I no longer had that choice, and furthermore, I had matured measurably in my spousal relationship. I had to find another manner of being to go forward stronger than when I had started. Conscious awareness was quintessential to my ability to transform our romantic relationship into a lasting friendship.

Friendships, like romantic relationships, can last a lifetime or they can end for any number of reasons. People are put on our paths at different times for different reasons. Not all friendships are meant to last an entire lifetime. Our friends tend to be a little bit like us, holding similar views, engaging in the same hobbies, and sharing the same preferences. We tend to have friends who agree with us and support our activities and interests. Our friends also tend to operate at a similar frequency to us. When one person changes his or her frequency (whether it is elevated or simply different), the friendship will show signs of strain and begin to change. These changes can look as mundane as having different ideals or interests, or more imaginative like taking the form of a new persona, association or vocation.

This phenomenon happens in romantic, family, and work relationships too.

The feelings associated with losing a friend are related to the change in ideas, actions, or interests of someone we thought we knew. Misunderstandings can occur that are often secondary to the inability to communicate effectively with one another. Perhaps someone can no longer hear you, for instance. Or perhaps you can no longer understand someone.

Our friendships evolve, just as we do.

I once lost a good friend. A beautiful person, and someone I loved. I know I loved her because the loss was deep enough that I felt it for more than twenty years. I suppose that love has never quite gone away. I never fully understood what happened between us. There wasn't a man or money, or a specific thing that broke our friendship, it was something else. Perhaps a lack of trust is what ended our friendship. After a while, I imagined it was some sort of misunderstanding, but rationalizing the loss did not make it less palpable.

The end of this special friendship was rather abrupt. I literally didn't know what was going on. I was too immature at the time to talk about it. I just felt thrown out. Done with. And it hurt.

Now as I look back, I see that everything was changing in my life in that moment. I had just gotten accepted into medical school a thousand miles away from the home I grew up in. I was embarking on a rigorous career, meeting new friends, and discovering different things. Now, more than two decades later, I have realized that every single relationship has changed remarkably from when I was in my early twenties. The relationship with myself, my relationships with family members, my friendships, and my relationships with professional colleagues all have evolved. No relationship has ever remained static.

Even though we may never fully understand the reasoning behind the changes that occur, they are somehow necessary in our actualization continuum. It is only more recently that I truly know the value of a good friendship. For this full life experience with friends, family, and lovers, I am forever grateful.

CHAPTER 17

Love, Sex, and Intimacy

Many people feel that first love is the best love. A first love is fearless because it is innocent. The first person you ever fall in love with hasn't hurt you yet, so your heart loves as intended, openly and honestly. There's a feeling of oneness without time.

When we are young, we do not know the pain of love lost, so we can love willingly and freely. As we experience more about life and feel the pain of loss, we begin to guard our hearts, sometimes closing them off altogether, so we no longer feel the pain. When we close our hearts due to pain, the exchange of mutual love cannot occur. The connection is lost. We cannot love another person. In closing our hearts, we unconsciously forbid others to love us.

Love is a core necessity of realizing the true self. Love and intimacy together create a union that establishes a wholeness between lives. This can be achieved with anyone. It does not matter whom you love so long as you have the experience of connected love.

Once in a while, when the moment is right, we meet an embodied being that we feel we have known throughout eternity. This connection is an endless love your heart will recognize immediately. The heart can see beyond appearances. It is only with the heart that you can see your truest love, as it looks beyond form and knows only the love energy. This immortal type of love has a palpable feeling to it and insists upon a powerful, yet quiet acquiescence, despite prevailing circumstances and our presence of mind. It does not make excuses. It is resolute and in the moment.

Soon enough the mind and the subjective eye get involved to have their say. It is inevitable. But meeting a person with whom you have shared an eternal love—perhaps from a connection you made in a past life—will be no accident. Regardless of how miraculous the unfolding, it will be no coincidence. To have this experience is an exquisite reminder of the way of the Multiverse where possibilities are boundless.

I met my eternal love on a day much like any other day. On this particular day, I had a job interview and did not have a single expectation when it came to love. But when my love walked into the room and introduced himself to me, I felt a foreign sensation in my chest. Before that moment, I had thought my heart was closed to love. What happened to me was not like a juvenile feeling of infatuation but like an electric spark resonating from the deepest recesses around my heart. A lightness came over me. I was having an awakening.

I tried my best to deny what this experience signified on that day and on the hundreds of days that have followed, but the truth of it has stayed with me for several years now. I've tried to talk myself out of it because of inconvenience, fear, and countless other reasons. I keep telling myself I am ready for this love, but apparently, it is not ready for me—otherwise an earthly relationship would manifest.

What has been most spectacular about recognizing the nature of this love is that I now can experience what seems impossible in my physical reality. I can now experience love in another dimension. I can pick up on the thoughts of the man I love and interact with him at a higher frequency in my dream state. This is an experience like no other, one I have never knowingly had with another living being.

On several occasions, my love and I have connected on the other side. In one instance, I was standing at what appeared to be a kitchen sink, drying dishes. Through the corner of my eye, I could see him coming toward me at an energetic pace that is not experienced on Earth. I was paralyzed in awe at having this moment with my love in a higher dimension. As soon as our energies touched, the vibrational release was that of eons letting go. It felt like the culmination of all existential interstellar bangs, melting away what remained of my earthly body. Love at this high frequency cannot be held in the physical form; the power of pure love is too sublime. We only can retain a residual memory of this highest form of love and are in constant pursuit of recapturing the feeling in our bodies when we make love.

The opportunity to again experience the highest love frequency is what is behind all manners of romantic physical acts. We would be misguided, however, to think that this frequency could be born out of a physical act alone. It is the love *energy* that creates such an immense feeling.

When love is absent from a physical sexual act, we do not approach the love frequency on an emotional level. In fact, on such an occasion intercourse can be draining to the body and lead to a soulful emptiness. We must first connect at the heart level to experience the love frequency. Only a fragment of the highest love energy resides within each of our physical bodies. Despite this, the consensual experience of connecting both physically and at the heart level reminds us of the immense power of pure love energy.

The intensity of feeling love at a higher frequency eclipses all physical experiences I've ever had. The love vibration surpasses all others; its power is unparalleled. This does not mean that there is nothing left to explore in the physical realm. What remains is the opportunity for a shared love experience and to have connectedness and intimacy with another awakened soul.

Love is more than a frequency; it is sheer beauty. It paints your perspective and can provide you comfort throughout your life's long and winding passage.

The physical dimension comes with limitations that are not present in the cosmic realms. Many travelers have sexual experiences of all varieties in different dimensions. These incidents are not worthy of mention and differ markedly from an unadulterated love experience. The same is true here on Earth in what we perceive as our real lives.

The feeling of love originates from the energy body. Love vibrates at the highest energetic frequency and cannot be exhausted. When love energy is exchanged, you are energized, not drained. You can never have or give too much love. It is the actions born out of the love feeling that can be misguided or taken in excess. The body allows us to show our love in a physical way. This expression has its own rhythm, power, and limits. The high-frequency love generated by the energy body is processed and interpreted by the mind, the heart, the gut, and the genitals.

The physical actions of exchanging love can unfold in spectacular ways. We show our feeling of energetic love by physically having a sexual experience. When a sexual act comes from the emotion of genuine love, the act is elevated to lovemaking. When we reach orgasm, it is only a glimpse of the highest love energy that is within us.

The highest orgasmic frequency is one that the physical body cannot tolerate. The full expression of love energy can be consummated only when we're out of the body.

Intimacy is very different from lovemaking or sex. Simply put, it is being with someone on the level of the energy body. Intimacy looks through the eye, beyond the physical form, and into the soul. It is when the light in me sees the light in you—and vice versa. It goes beyond the flesh and is often sorely lacking in purely physical relationships. A genuine love connection does not occur in the absence of intimacy.

Intimacy can be lost with breach of trust or loss of integrity. You cannot really know someone if you neglect to see the whole person. You can, of course, have a sexual experience without love or intimacy. That is, however, the lowest form of sexual experience and not sustainable in a healthy way. On a basic human level, you cannot have high-frequency love without intimacy. You must find some way to connect with another being to experience the intimate love vibration.

Intimacy can occur between acquaintances, friends, and family members, as well as in romantic relationships. All relationships are built on a foundation of trust. Intimacy emerges from that foundation.

Perhaps you have been hurt and think it will be too painful to open your heart to love again. I encourage you to do your best to heal so you may try. At the end of the day, love is all there is. It takes letting go of the past to move on. Look only for genuine love relationships when moving forward. Not only romantic love but the whole spectrum of love. Engage with everyone you come to know in the spirit of love. Break the cycle of entering personal relationships out of the fear of being alone or for a desire for money, status, or title. Love for love's sake.

Seeing the beauty in others allows the beauty in us to be witnessed as well. Having the love experience is vitally important and informs our ability to transcend Earth's third dimension—as love is the lightest and highest of all frequencies. It is also of the utmost importance to allow yourself to be loved again.

Know that you are not alone on your journey. A hardened or closed heart turns to stone, precluding intimacy and ultimately crumbling under the pressures of life. Open your heart and trust again. You are wiser now. Be fearless once again. You won't be disappointed. The world appears different through the eyes of love. The wonder comes back, the world comes alive again. Feeling once more can be scary, of course, but it is worth overcoming your fear to find this type of fulfillment in life.

Every living being deserves to feel love. Love, after all, is the divine frequency behind all of creation. What living creature does not thirst for water? Who in life does not yearn for love?

CHAPTER 18

Gender and the Energy Body

We are born into a rather rigid human body complex with gender apparatus (a penis or a vagina) that designates us as either male or female. The physical traits and hormonal systems of the two genders do not allow for many possibilities in terms of human expression. The human body is an inflexible construct often restricting us into defined societal roles. Our life energy, on the other hand, is neither strictly male nor female but rather fluid in composition encompassing a wide array of potentials.

Energy doesn't have a specific gender. As the conduit of our consciousness, however, the energy body does have tendencies and preferences. The energy body also possesses latent memories of its past experiences and lives that were experienced in differing gender assignments. The energy body is an emotional body that has feelings and a mixture of both masculine and feminine energy. It also encompasses intangible qualities that cannot be defined in terms of gender characteristics.

Remember, the life energy contained in any single embodied individual is an infinitesimal fraction of the total Source energy from which the individual comes. The complete energy from which a body operates could not be contained in a single physical form due to its overwhelming power, complexity, and scale. Our earthly bodies are minuscule in proportion to the whole of our beingness.

The diversity and enormity of life forms that exist in our shared Universe are often denied by the human mind. This multiplicity is to be experienced, like consciousness itself. It cannot be fully explained or strictly defined. The Universe is inconceivably vast whereby the life forms on Earth represent only a minute region of an immense territory. However, Earth life is not trivial. Our smallness in the scope of all that *is* does not imply insignificance.

The complete life energy that each of us is a part of is splintered into many life forms around the cosmos and spans many dimensions. This allows the whole to mature and eventually return to the Source. In this broader context of who we are, it is understandable that being relegated to either a male or female physical form is both limiting and stifling.

Throughout the ages, society has reinforced the rigid construct of gender and sexual identity by assigning roles and acceptable ways of being. Behavior falling outside of the limiting gender construct determined by a given society has been punishable by death. We even go as far as assigning gender to colors and objects, although there is nothing intrinsically masculine or feminine about a specific color or shape. The colors we can see are the light frequencies that the human eye can register.

We are conditioned to think about colors as masculine or feminine, but they are energetic frequencies much like our own energy bodies. Within each energy body is a combination of feminine and masculine qualities. Similarly, physical bodies of both genders secrete a mixture of estrogen and testosterone.

That said, the fluidity of the energy body is not well represented in the stringent male-female paradigm.

When someone doesn't fit squarely into the societal ideal of male or female, some people experience fear. Fear in this context is learned. It is a reaction to an unmet expectation. We are taught to expect a man to look and behave in a specific way and a woman to look and behave in a certain way. When a person does not meet our expectations for their assigned gender role, we have a feeling that something is wrong. We generally learn how to react to this feeling by observing the behavior of others or by being taught what we should do when we feel a certain way when we are still children. As adults, we can change our responses by educating our minds.

The fluid expression of gender is not something to be feared. It is something to be witnessed and accepted. The mutability of gender expression reminds some beings of their own energetic tendencies. If a being is uncomfortable with his or her own tendencies, he or she may go on to process the reminder violently because there is an inherent rejection of self. For others, variations in gender expression are simply understood on a soul level and accepted despite societal norms.

It is unfortunate that at this point in human history we still have difficulty accepting that there is greater complexity to the expression of human sexuality than just the heterosexual male-female relationship. The fact of the matter is that we all have the capacity to love anyone and anything. Once people can see past the body, realizing that it is only a shell housing a soul, they can begin to understand that it is the energy body which is the true source of attraction. The force that draws us together comes from within.

I have come to understand that the labels we place on each other do not matter at all. What is most important for anyone having a life on Earth is to experience it. If you are a soul who is uncomfortable in your given body, this speaks only to the complexity of your beauty and strength. It is not easy being *different* in the eyes of other people, whether that difference is in gender identity or in racial identities to which some cling. To be yourself inside and out is to be brave. It is hindsight that will show those who have judged the error of their ways. And that judgment will have to be transmuted before the ascension of that person can occur. This stands true even when the judgment is of yourself.

The energy body is not bound to any human construct. It has an ancient past and an infinite future and must remain malleable to withstand the experiences yet to come.

CHAPTER 19
Children

Every human being is born of a woman and arrives on Earth as a helpless infant. Yet, babies are conscious, genius, and powerful at birth. Their authority is so resolute that anyone in their presence stops to takes notice, stands at attention, and hurries to serve. People instinctively know that they are witnessing love in its purest form. Never will you see more adults hustling about to serve than when they're in the presence of a newly descended being. Newborns covertly remind us of our descent from the Universal edict.

At birth, we are still conscious and emotionally open to the force of the Multiverse. The veil of consciousness remains transparent for a period. With the birth of a child, we are reminded of the greatness of our physical creation. Early childhood is a special time, even for the most ancient of energy beings. In the mind of a child, everything is possible. Adults permit children to remember unseen energy beings and to dream untethered. This tolerance allows children's veils to remain drawn back and open to higher consciousness.

By the time a child reaches elementary school age, the amnestic veil that shields its consciousness is opacified. The purpose of having an amnestic veil is to allow new arrivals to fully experience Earth life without being burdened or confused by the knowledge of their past lives. The life energy embodied within the child must start over again and begin a lifelong journey of remembering through introspection. Forgetting the higher realms is also encouraged by adults who insist that children "grow up."

If we retained our immortal knowledge and fully understood that we are only having a physical existence that amounts to a blink of an eye compared with the age of the Universe, we would be less likely to learn and mature our eternal souls. It's like knowing what's going on behind the scenes of a magic show. Once you know how a trick is done, the experience ceases to amaze you. You are not inspired to learn more or to do your work of introspection. You are less driven to explore and have varied life experiences.

I have had several philosophical discussions with friends about what it would be like to go back in time and relive certain events while retaining current knowledge. We all agreed that we could not have had the same experiences if we took our current wisdom back to an earlier age. Your first love might never be actualized if you already knew what was going to happen. All of those "first" experiences would somehow be muted, or perhaps avoided entirely. The world would soon lose its wonder.

Children, moreover, are not really children, despite the way we perceive them. Yes, they are new to their bodies, but the life energy of a child is as ancient as Source energy itself. Some children retain the memories of past incarnations during the early part of their human existence. It is not unusual for a new baby to be the embodiment of a recently departed relative. In this instance, the dead relative was likely unable to transcend Earth's third dimension and so was given another opportunity to elevate his or her frequency while again embodied as a human.

This is not true for all new arrivals, but it is not uncommon. Soul groups tend to travel together for millennia. Soul groups are like families in the ethereal planes. As such, it is preferable that a mother knows the soul of her child before birth. It makes for a smoother transition and facilitates physical bonding. If the new baby is not a part of the legacy soul group of the mother or father, there may be difficulties in the familial relationship.

There are billions of life energies that are too dense to transcend near-Earth dimensions. These energies essentially cue up in perpetuity to have another chance at maturing their energy bodies on Earth. Some beings agree to reenter Earth life under desperate circumstances and lead very troubled lives as a result. The goal of incarnation is to have an Earth experience that enables us to eventually graduate from Earth School.

Our spiritual amnesia serves a purpose, like all things in life. The idea is that we come full circle: from birth to juvenile amnesia, self-discovery, lifting the veil, and knowing again. However, the majority of people get stuck somewhere in the middle of the cycle, never emerging from the densest emotional energy to know again who they really are at the end of their human incarnations. Each lifetime is designed to teach us what we failed to learn during our past lives. Unfortunately, too many of us die in fear and confusion only to have to do it all over again.

When our life energy remains heavy with anger, fear, and disillusionment, we do not transcend our earthly existence at death because we are not as enlightened as when we arrived.

It is important to remember that the death of the physical body is an illusion of the third dimension. We truly never die, we simply transform. Thereby, grief is not necessary. We do not mourn the caterpillar that becomes the butterfly. We admire the beauty of the transformation.

Earth life has irrefutable magnificence. It is truly a rare gift to have an embodied life experience here. However, the third-dimensional Earth experience is not all that there is. Imagine if, as a species, we were only able to live to the age of eighteen. We would then die some sort of dramatic physical death only to be directed back in line to be born again and do it over. This would seem a bit crazy, knowing that there is so much more to life that comes after eighteen that would never be experienced. We would essentially just be getting potty-trained and going through primary school repeatedly. Who in good conscience under these conditions would choose this existence?

I raise this scenario to extrapolate it to the broader third-dimensional existence we are now living. There are numerous other dimensions and embodied experiences to have. Why get repeatedly stuck in a dense third dimension? Earth is a remarkable place, but it is also treacherous and at times it is daunting to come full circle here. Do the work required of you to elevate your frequency now so that when your physical death comes, you are ready. Know that there is more, infinitely more, to learn and discover after your life here on Earth completes.

Some parents will have the experience of losing a child. The intensity of pain in such a circumstance is likely stronger than the grief of losing any other loved one in life. The parent-child relationship carries weight. It is endowed with unconditional love. Parents have the inherent responsibly of guardianship for a child, keeping the child safe from bodily and emotional harm. Parents do not own their children but are charged with guiding them through their earthly existence. Souls that are quick to depart, arrive on Earth for all sorts of reasons. Some come as teachers to their parents where others find the confines of the physical body too stifling and choose to leave as a result.

What remains unrevealed at birth is the nature of the parent-child contract created on the other side of the veil. Neither children nor their parents will remember. If a child should die before its parents, the parents' hearts may be burdened by a heavy amount of grief and blame (aimed either toward themselves or others, depending on whom they feel was responsible for the physical death). Their loss is compounded by their general lack of understanding about the purpose of the child's life, or their own lives. As a collective, we are too focused on the physicality of being to truly comprehend the duality of being. The pain that is felt when a soul departs as a child is an experience in unto itself to be transformed. All the emotions we possess are to be experienced, no matter how unpalatable we perceive them to be. As adults, we are largely unaware and hold a lack of understanding of our own soul growth. Therefore, we believe we are being punished when we experience pain.

Some embodied beings are like flames that burn hot for an instant in time, whereas others are like flames that burn cooler and longer, over an extended embodiment. We can't begin to understand all that has happened in past incarnations. This information is, however, available in the Akashic Records. The Akashic Records are like a supreme spiritual database containing all of the intentions, thoughts, actions, and deeds of every being ever incarnated in physical form. Your personal records can be accessed and viewed while in your light body. There are also enlightened people on Earth who can assist you with such access. We cannot know the full context of our current incarnations from a purely physical perspective. What looks like a tragedy to us may be predetermined and necessary for the evolution of the soul of the child who has died.

Remember, there is a cosmic balance imperative. Everything in existence moves toward energetic balance. The agreements made before incarnation to balance inequities of the past can look like wars, diseases, accidents, or natural disasters. We cannot fully comprehend the path taken by others throughout past eons nor can we know how the balance is to be paid during their current embodiments. There are no victims in life, just misunderstandings about the totality of existence.

What can provide us with some comfort when a child dies is knowing that the child is not alone. Know that the life energy of a previously embodied child is handled gently and with great care. The child's energy lands in a comfortable dimension where it is surrounded by many guides and teachers, and where the frequency is best suited to its soul's evolution at that moment.

Departed souls always land in frequencies consistent with their vibrations at the end of their physical lives. Tormented souls, like souls of children and adults who have had a traumatic passing, are cared for in special dimensions that allow these souls to heal before moving into another embodiment. Much like hospitals and places of respite on Earth, there are dedicated celestial infirmaries for injured souls. The time construct outside of the third dimension does not exist, so the amount of *time* a soul spends in respite cannot be accurately compared.

Interestingly, an energy body does not retain all its memories of the most recent Earth life forever, just as you may not remember what you had for lunch last Tuesday. Some memories are forgotten, and others are retained until the next incarnation.

Holding on to heavy past emotions prevents energetic flight. A soul will not elevate in frequency so long as it holds on to dense emotions, like pain, bitterness, anger, and fear. This is true for the souls of the departed as well as the souls of the embodied who remain behind when a loved one dies.

The purpose of an embodiment is to have the experience, to grow from it, and finally, to transcend it. As harsh as it may sound, the parents whose children have died are tasked with forgiveness and letting go. Letting go does not mean you are abandoning your child's memory. You will still love and miss your child. It is the pain that resides in your heart center which must be released. Guilt, anger, and fear must also be released. With the loss of a child, parents are called, on a soul level, to trust in powers unseen and in doing so transform themselves.

In very painful situations, instead of just asking *Why did this happen?* ask yourself *Why am I experiencing this? What is there to learn in this situation?* Begin the introspective process of self-examination. You can also begin to ask your higher self for understanding and what it is you can do to transmute the pain.

When it comes to the death of a child, a family can hold the density of pain throughout their entire existence here on Earth. The pain will then spill over into every aspect of their lives. There is no easy way through something like this. However, the introspective process has the potential within it to bring you peace.

The work of introspection also opens the possibility to communicate with a departed soul in your dream state, the natural time for the soul to explore multiple dimensions and to heal.

When I have a painful or otherwise stressful situation to address with my higher self, I set the intention as I am lying down to sleep at night. In the state where I am just about to doze off, when there is a loosened awareness of my physical reality, at that moment I begin a conversation with myself. I ask for clarity from my guides. I set the intention to communicate with the recently departed and ask for a memory and a renewed sense of understanding upon awakening. This process never fails to provide me with a restful sleep and sense of peace.

I do not always remember what occurred on a soul level every night, but I do feel a shift when an issue has been resolved. Resolution in the ethereal planes is not always immediate on Earth in the setting of the dense time construct that you and I experience. But you will have a knowing from within that everything is going to be okay. You may not understand why you feel lighter after nightly introspective exercises like this one, but you will be able to feel the difference.

The difference you feel is the energetic shift required to move you forward.

Star Children

A great many children born today are hypersensitive to their surroundings. These children are in many ways retaining a translucent veil when it comes to their ability to perceive higher consciousness. They are populating the Earth to assist in the upward vibrational shift of both the planet and its inhabitants. They have a special relationship with animals, the environment, and other beings. Their sensitivity to the conditions here can lead to *disorders* like autism and attention deficit hyperactivity disorder, and severe allergies. Due to their sensitivity, some of these special children experience deep depression and anxiety. They also have unique abilities to create, display understanding, express empathy, and show compassion beyond their years.

Many possess extraordinary intelligence, psychic skills, and artistic talent. Children of this kind began appearing on Earth in masses during the early 1970s and are known as *Indigo children.*

Now grown, the Indigos are often parents of the newest generation of highly sensitive beings who are known as *Crystal children* or *Star children.* The Crystal children tend to have an affinity for crystals, rocks, or even dirt. They may decide to become vegetarians in childhood due to their empathy and love for animals. The Star children sense that they come from other parts of the galaxy. All extra-conscious children have a feeling of not fitting in and intolerance for inauthenticity. They are older souls with great wisdom who can see through human constructs and have been called to the Earth to assist with the ascension of the planet and its people. Some Indigos, Stars, and Crystals may refer to themselves as *lightworkers.*

Highly sensitive and connected beings have inhabited the Earth over the millennia. These are the same beings who have brought us past advancements in agriculture, industry, technology, and spirituality. There is a preponderance of modern-era lightworkers in service to humanity as the Earth is preparing to ascend out of the third dimension. Earth's ascension will be discussed further in Chapter 24.

CHAPTER 20

Powers

Awakening to consciousness has benefits beyond multidimensional travel that can be experienced while still embodied. Many gifts associated with conscious awareness are gained by the elevation of our vibrational frequencies. The gift of awareness provides us with the opportunity to consciously ascend the third dimension after death. But we don't have to wait years or for the moment of death for the rewards of our introspective work to kick in. There is another reason to want to elevate your frequency as soon as possible. While still on Earth, elevated consciousness heightens your senses and revives our latent powers. Powers can range from sharper intuition to seeing auras, telepathy, telekinetic abilities, and the ability to heal the physical body.

All powers revealed through your conscious awakening were always a part of you but were rendered dormant until the moment of your awakening. Some awakened souls among us will discover that they have greater empathic sensitivities, the ability to communicate with animals, clairvoyance, or clairaudience, just to mention a few powers that could emerge. Consciousness will provide them with new perspectives on just about every aspect of their lives: knowledge of complex issues and the ability to tap into higher realms of understanding.

As you make your journey into conscious awareness, ask your higher self what powers will be revealed to you. Ask to *be* in your power. You will soon be able to track the progression of your frequency elevation based on the revelation of your innate powers. No single individual could possess every power, but the ones you do have latent within you will be more than enough to change your life forever.

The first awakened power I experienced was the ability to leave my body spontaneously. I came to learn that my soul has long been a multidimensional traveler. I was tasked with remembering this aspect of myself during my awakening. Since the activation of the soul-traveling abilities, I began to notice changes in my sense of hearing. I began to hear different tones and shifts of ambient sound frequencies. I first noticed a change one afternoon during a nap. I was used to hearing static when things were quiet around me, kind of like the sound of white noise. Then one day, I heard a rather loud crack in my ears followed by audible tones. The tones were not bothersome at all, I was only surprised at actually hearing them. My first thought was that I might be developing tinnitus, but I recalled from my medical school training that patients found tinnitus to be quite disruptive and, in many instances, it was brought on by aspirin use. I was neither bothered by the tones nor using aspirin. I just accepted the tones and began to intently listen to them to discern if perhaps, I was receiving some sort of message.

I am still not altogether sure what the tones mean but I suspect they are a related to me being in tune with the Universe. I have now had the ear tones for more than six years and continue to hear tonal shifts every now and again. I feel the tonal shifts are related to the changes in my vibrational frequency.

Over the past several years, I have also awakened my abilities to see auras, not just around people but surrounding ordinary objects. I have seen a vibrant green aura around the yoga mat of my favorite instructor. I have seen auras in trees, photographs, furniture, electronics, and just about anything else imaginable. Aura viewing for me has also come with the ability to feel the energetic signature of an individual whose inner light I am observing. This ability to feel the energy of others has allowed me to have greater compassion for all of humanity.

During my first year of multidimensional travel, I had my first Reiki healing session while on retreat outside of my home state. Several months later, when I was back home in Atlanta, I did a Google search for Reiki healers in my area. I booked an appointment online with a healer I had never met. When I arrived for my appointment, I signed a waiver and entered the room for my healing session. I mentioned to my healer that I was experiencing stress at home and chronic low back pain, which was the reason for my appointment. She began performing Reiki on me and I could feel my energy body leaving my physical body. I was very pleased with this because any time my energy moved out, I felt renewed and peaceful upon my return to the physical.

When the session ended, my healer sounded a bell and told me not to move. I was unaware that during the session she had been placing many stones and crystals around my body. She left the room and came back with a cup of water and appeared visibly shaken. She removed dozens of stones surrounding my hands and feet and asked me to take a seat at the small wooden desk that was in the room and handed me my water. She commented, "I don't know how to tell you this but during the session I feared that I was going to *lose you* on the table." She admitted that she would not have known how to get me back. I reassured her that I could always find my way back to my body and she didn't need to worry about that.

The healer went on to say that in her twenty-plus years of practicing Reiki, she had never encountered an energy like mine, which she called an *ancient energy*. She continued by saying that if I ever wanted to learn to move energy, she would teach me.

It was nearly eight months later when I went back to her as a student to learn how to move energy and receive my Reiki attunements. In a period of two and a half years, I received my master attunements in Reiki and now practice energy healing with private clients. Every Reiki master has different energetic powers and ways of practicing. My attunements have allowed me to communicate telepathically with the soul of my clients during energy sessions. I am a conduit for healing energy that is in only the highest good of the receiver. I am now able to heal my son's eczema using Reiki without the use of either over-the-counter or prescription medications. I also now use Reiki on myself.

In 1997, during my first year of medical school, I developed idiopathic angioedema. Angioedema is a condition of disfiguring swelling of the face, hands, feet or virtually any part of the body and is related to but different than hives. *Idiopathic* is a term that refers to a condition having no known medical cause. The cause of my angioedema was the stress of not being on my rightful path in life.

I experienced angioedema for nearly twenty years before I got control of it. My conscious awakening helped but it was the use of Reiki healing that has allowed me to be rid of it for good. When I am about to have an episode of swelling, I can feel it coming on. Before my conscious awakening, I would start cursing the situation, dreading the next eighteen to twenty-four hours of irritation and disfigurement. As I began to become more aware of the interplay of my soul and physical body, when I would feel the swelling coming on I would stop in my tracks, no matter what I was doing, and address it. I would ask myself *What is my body trying to tell me?* Without fail, I would hear my soul telling me about some trivial worry I had going on inside of me. In that instant, I would acknowledge it and let go of the fear. I would apologize to my body for the internal stress I was causing it, and I would then use Reiki to immediately resolve any swelling that was forming. Before long, I could nip it in the bud. Now, before the angioedema can fully flare, I acknowledge the cause with conscious introspection and use healing energy to reverse and resolve it completely.

As you begin to wake up to consciousness, notice your latent powers awakening too. Realize your true powers will be instrumental in unfolding your rightful path in life.

CHAPTER 21

Thoughts

Energy is the essence of everything in existence, both seen and unseen, including our thoughts. Thoughts carry tremendous power. They are active, transformative energetic entities. Thoughts in the metaphysical context are known as *thought forms*. The Multiverse has a process for bringing thought forms into physical existence. In English, this dimensional exchange is known as *manifestation*.

Your thoughts do not go unnoticed. They are heard as requests by your higher self and Source energy. The Multiverse responds to the vibrational signature accompanying the thought with in-kind manifestation because it wants to give you what you want. The key is that your thoughts must be aligned with how you really feel. Very often, we think we want something and yet harbor sabotaging feeling in our hearts. We may think we really want a lot of money, for example, only to be feeling frustration, lack, or inadequacy in our hearts. Such a misalignment of thoughts and feelings produces confusing results in our physical reality.

Typically, we put most of our energy into things that we really want. The process includes creating a thought form and putting actions and language behind it to increase its power.

The more attention we give and the more actions we take to realize an idea, the faster it comes to fruition. Ideas require our attention. Attention is another form of energy—one that gives an idea momentum.

Everything observed by us is changed in some way through the act of the observation itself. Observation is a way of bringing something into your awareness. And when there is awareness, something seemingly miraculous occurs.

Many of us have had the experience of buying a new car. Prior to the purchase, we do research and begin observing cars to determine what features we want. Once we buy the car, we notice how prevalent that car now seems. It appears that we are seeing the same car all the time everywhere we go. You see, the vehicles similar to the new car were always there; they were just existing outside our awareness. Focusing your thoughts and putting them into action increases your awareness.

Energetically, what is happening when you observe something? Once an object or experience you desire enters your awareness, a cosmic acceleration of its manifestation ensues. This is true for the higher frequency things you think about as well as for the lower frequency thoughts you have. You can manifest cars all around you. Similarly, if you spend your time perseverating on how things aren't working out for you or how terribly annoying something is, you unconsciously bring the difficulty and irritation into your awareness. You will begin to perceive that the annoying thing is occurring all around you.

Every physical thing in existence began as an idea in someone's mind, as a thought form. I am not just referring to human-made objects. It is not just embodied beings who think about what can be brought to fruition. The Planet Earth itself was thought into existence by the greater collective consciousness of the Multiverse.

Thought energy originates in the energy body. Thoughts are processed and rationalized by humans in their physical minds. The Multiverse processes thoughts in its own way. Many of the brightest ideas conceived by human beings are the result of direct instruction received from the cosmos through the connection between the physical self and the higher self. This is when flashes of genius occur.

Often people wake up in the early morning hours with ingenious ideas that were captured while they slept. Many, unfortunately, cannot tell you how they came to have their epiphanies because they are unconscious to the activity of their higher selves. But individuals who recognize their dual nature and connection to Source can consciously direct their thought forms to their higher selves and manifest freely. Others who have lost awareness of their divine connection can toil for decades or even a lifetime before a complete idea is brought into physical reality.

In the process of writing *The Duality of Being*, I became stuck. Many refer to this as writer's block. A week or two went by when I could not think of a single word to put on the pages. I began doing Google searches looking for advice on how to overcome writer's block. I thought perhaps I needed a muse. I found several anecdotal solutions, but none resonated with me. As a new author, I did not have a pattern or system for my book writing. I then decided to ask my higher self what to do.

That night as I was going to bed, I would state my intention to my higher self using my inner voice. I would ask for inspiring words to allow certain chapters of my book to resonate with my future readers. And I made a point to capture any ideas that came to me promptly. I kept a notepad on my nightstand and another on the bathroom counter as I would often get ideas while lying in bed or taking a shower. I also would record my thoughts on my mobile phone whenever they would appear. If I was cooking dinner for example and an inspiring idea would enter my head, I would reach for my phone or a sticky note and jot it down. Within one month, I wrote more than 30,000 words.

I never forced myself to write if the inspiration wasn't there. But if I didn't write one day, I would set the definite intention to write the next day. I had enough awareness to thank my higher self for providing me the resources and understanding to write these chapters.

Writing a manuscript is like bringing anything to fruition. When I think about purchasing a new car, buying a new home, or going on a relaxing vacation, I begin actively thinking about it. I research it and take measured steps to realize my desire. I put dates of departure on my calendar even before I purchase airline tickets. I also describe to myself how I will feel when everything comes together. I have noticed that when I set an intention in this manner, I tend to get 80–90 percent of what I have said I wanted.

I don't spare any details when describing what I wish to accomplish to my higher self. No desire is too big for the Multiverse to fulfill. I make lists by hand or I use digital media.

It is important to realize that the Multiverse is designed to give you what you want. Don't hesitate to ask for everything you need or something even better. You must, however, do the work of manifestation by aligning your thoughts with the feelings in your heart. Crossing your fingers and hoping and wishing is not enough. For although having thoughts makes things possible, it is the actions and feeling behind an idea that enable those things to appear in the physical realm.

You see, there is a universal law governing creation that is always active and in perfect working order. When we fail to manifest rightly, we must look to ourselves to find the error or block in our vibrational signature.

Take the example of Newton's third law of motion applied to aerodynamics. Understanding how this law works has allowed aviators, scientist, engineers, and inventors to successfully put airplanes and rockets in the air. If a plane falls from the sky, we would not believe for a single moment that Newton's third law has suddenly failed. Leonardo da Vinci aptly remarked that nature never breaks her own laws. Similarly, we would look to the body of the physical plane to find the defect in design or functionality.

The same holds for the universal law of manifestation. When manifestation does not work as intended, we must look to the physical being attempting the manifestation and investigate the energetic blocks or design flaws in the approach to creation. Frequently we find incongruencies between the thought forms projected and the vibrational frequencies radiating from the heart center. Ultimately, there must be an alignment with what we think, speak, and feel to create that which we truly desire.

In the process of creation, some people become paralyzed with indecision. Not knowing what initial steps to take, they fail to take any steps at all.

For your ease, here is a simple process.

1. Imagine your future self already having that which is only a desire today. Decide for yourself what it is that you truly want. What would it feel like to have what you desire most? Write down your desires *and* feelings.

2. Reflect on steps you could take to arrive in the future you just created for yourself, holding onto that high vibrational feeling of love.

3. Bravely take the first of these steps. It may be as easy as filling out an application, making a call, or writing down a plan of action.

4. To overcome any fear you might have, ask yourself, *What is the worst that could happen if I take this first step?* It may be rejection you fear or perhaps even your own success. Know that you can survive any rejection and continue taking forward steps. Always examine feelings that appear to be holding you back. Ask yourself, *What is this heavy feeling about?* to begin the process of self-awareness. Several publishers refused to publish the book you are now reading. Don't let anyone outside of you thwart your dreams.

5. Remind yourself regularly that the actions you take now are the precursors of your future life experience.

6. Repeatedly align your high vibrational feelings with your goals. Be certain that your goals are aligned with your passion and are worthy of your power.

7. Move boldly into your future. It is what you are born to do.

CHAPTER 22

The Future

The future is forever unfolding from actions taken in the present moment. The details of its unfolding, however, are not at all certain until they tangibly happen. Future thought forms must "cross" the Point of Now to come into physical form. As you may recall from Chapter 11, "Time," the *Point of Now* is my term for the convergence of past, present, and future. In higher-frequency dimensions all events are happening at the same "moment." The barrier that must be crossed is not really a two-dimensional line, like a fence. It's more like a gathering force that reaches conditions of heightened potential, at which point a probability becomes a reality.

For a thought form to cross the Point of Now, actions must be taken to support the thoughts and intentions you are putting into the Multiverse. Many forces are in motion to create the future, as the fates and lives of many are intertwined in ways inconceivable. Some manifestations can occur instantaneously. Others take a bit longer because there are more factors involved. Your clarity, consistency of effort, and emotion are essential for purposeful manifestation to occur.

When we think about what we want to achieve, acquire, or experience, a new energetic form is created and sent into the

Multiverse. Thoughts are powerful things, but they require concerted energy to take form somewhere in the Multiverse. Giving energy to a thought means nurturing it. When you have an idea that you want to bring alive, you will actively think about it, speak about it, and begin sharing it with others. The act of sharing an idea gives power to the intention as additional people begin to apply their energy to the manifestation of the same idea as you. Your thoughts and feeling about an idea must be in alignment (as must those within a group of collaborators) or you will begin to materialize confusing outcomes. If you have a bright idea, and yet, in your heart, believe that it can never work, that it's too ambitious, or too difficult to accomplish, you will experience what your inner feelings are resonating. You will find yourself working very hard and exploring options that never work out.

The biggest and best ideas must be approached from a heart-focused perspective, and from your faith that everything is possible. Lay out all possibilities that you can think of when you are setting your intentions but also leave yourself open to every possibility you are unable to conceive in the moment. Allow yourself to accept the possibilities you have imagined yet be open to discover options that are even better than you can imagine.

Don't be too rigid with what you believe the Multiverse can deliver. And don't underestimate your very own powers of manifestation. There is literally an entire Universe connected to the true self that is housed inside of you. You are divine in terms of perfection and creation and an infinity among greater infinities.

The physical body has a brain that processes thoughts so that they can be interpreted in a physical context. The energy of the Multiverse must act on those thoughts in some way. This omnipotent force cannot engage with our every mental contemplation. The mind tends to endlessly chatter, so the Universe relies on our heart energy to convey a purer form of these messages. It is vitally important that the great ideas we hope and intend to manifest carry the energy signal of love. Love is the root frequency of the heart's vibration because it is the energy signature that resonates most intensely in the Multiverse. Manifestation is one of the key purposes why the heart is designed as it is—far beyond pumping blood through the circulatory system.

We are directly connected to the Multiverse and its Source energy through the vibrations of our heart center. A high-frequency intention coming from an open heart is heard clearly throughout the cosmos.

When we dream big, powerful thought forms begin to manifest the future within the field of creation. Although the future is realized from moment to moment, the event line of the future extends further out when it is exposed to multiple high-frequency thoughts and ideas. The further out the event line stretches, the more your future is already formulated and can be anticipated to manifest tangibly. When you have expansive thought forms and begin planning for the future, those thought forms begin to lay down a path for you. This probable future further solidifies from moment to moment as physical actions occur, further supporting future thoughts and ideas. As elements of the thought forms begin to materialize, this is when we see our desires coming to fruition.

Many actions are required to formulate an intention in a distant future. However, the future path for each of us begins to be laid down in the ethereal plane when our clear thoughts and intentions resonate through our heart center. The Multiverse then "hears" the frequency of the heart and begins to create the events that shape a corresponding future. The probability of an idea coming to fruition in the future depends on the power of the thought form and the authenticity of the intention behind it.

Creating your future is a form of manifestation. We get better at manifesting when we understand how the future is created and how ideas become *real,* as we understand reality in our 3D world. Know that thoughts and ideas are indeed real. Understanding the power of thoughts should encourage us to monitor our thoughts carefully. When a negative or dense thought enters your awareness, it is best to release it immediately. This can be done by replacing the doubtful thought and weighted feeling associated with it, with a higher vibrational feeling.

Imagine you are auditioning for an artistic production of your choosing (for instance, a play or a concert). Even though you do your very best, you leave the audition with feelings of doubt, reliving and criticizing your every move in your head. The energy of your critical thoughts drains you and undermines your confidence. We have every confidence in the world of realizing precisely everything we *do not* want. Negative mind chatter never serves you well.

You can transform your reality in situations like this one by doing your very best at the audition and then telling yourself that you've done all that you can — releasing the rest to your higher self and the beneficence of the Universe. In doing so, you release rigid thoughts about what you think the outcome should be. You open yourself up to all possibilities, not just those related to the audition you just completed. Elevating your thinking raises your vibrational frequency overall. You will also genuinely feel better about just about everything you do when you approach individual goals in this way.

At the end of the day, you may not get that part or gig. But notice how you feel in the presence of divine energy vs. the anguish you would have likely put yourself through in your prior mindset. There are endless possibilities for you. Open yourself to the prospect of receiving them. When one pathway is closed to you, another one is already awaiting your arrival.

There is an order to the Multiverse, a universal law. Trust that if a certain job, relationship, deal, or [fill in the blank] does not work out, know that there is something even better that is possible for you. Know this with every fiber of your being.

In this life, there are no accidents or coincidences. Trust yourself enough to create your future in presence of mind and with some sense peace about you. Understand that your choices and feelings in the present moment lay down the path that's unwinding as your future.

Your choices in the present moment set the future into motion. In life, we cannot know with absolution what the future holds as the Multiverse creates infinite possibilities. If we program our minds to accept just a few possibilities, then only the probable outcomes are predictable. The mind likes to know what to expect so it will send thought forms that support predictable and comfortable results. If, however, you are truly open to receiving all the possibilities the Multiverse has to offer, you will experience wonders far beyond your current imagination. The future will remain a mystery that you will have the pleasure of discovering as it brilliantly unfolds.

Open your heart to the expanse of the Multiverse, understanding that there is no order of difficulty in creation. The big is as easy to manifest as the small. The Multiverse is an all-knowing creative entity connected directly to the Source of all that *is*. We resonate with the Multiverse and ultimately with the Source when we dream big and lead with our hearts. The vibrational frequency of a joyous heartbeat most closely reflects the frequency of the force of the Multiverse.

Allow your mind to do its job and then get out of your own way. Allow all that can be. Collectively, we tend to fear the future because it is not certain and full of unknowns. Don't let your egoic mind or the spoils of doubt diminish your life experience to the limited expression of the most predictable of outcomes. Let go of all fear of the unknown and embrace your inner power. You are a child of God and by universal decree, you are a creator. Predictability is a trap of the egoic mind that has held humankind back for ages.

Be open to all that *is*. An expansive state of being elevates the frequency of the energy body by leaps and bounds, paving the way for emotional maturity and spiritual enlightenment. Know that the Multiverse wants you to have all that you desire. Let the soul go to work for you by sending thought forms at the height of the love frequency, then letting go of what you think should happen. By doing this, expect to be amazed.

CHAPTER 23

Sentience

Everything in existence is pure energy at its core. And it is the energy body of a living thing, no matter how small, that is the source of its consciousness. Even the most minute of particles that are the building blocks of larger atoms, such as quarks and leptons, have energy bodies and therefore possess consciousness. Every particle in the material Universe is in a constant state of motion and therefore can be said to have life. This is just as true for particles that compose inanimate objects, like rocks and furniture, as it is for animate creatures, like trees and giraffes. If we can imagine everything within knowable existence having mass, no matter how minute, then we can begin to understand that everything in knowable existence has consciousness.

All energetic life, in some way, holds consciousness. A rock may not have what we identify as human consciousness, but the rock indeed has consciousness because, at its elemental level, the rock is made of physical matter, which possesses energy. If we take the example of a common tree that is growing in the ground and flourishing in the presence of soil, sunlight and rain, we view this as being alive. Like other complex organisms, this tree is made up of billions, even trillions of individual cells and molecules. Within each cell are microorganelles undergoing active processes of metabolism.

At an even more microscopic level, beyond the subcellular processes of the tree, we understand that there is an energetic substrate that supports the physical manifestation of the tree. This substrate underlies the genetic code that determines how the tree takes shape and functions. From the genotype, the tree expresses its unique phenotype—its physical characteristics. The building blocks of an organism's genetic code are alive with consciousness and arrange themselves in elaborate sequences.

If we look deeper still into the atomic particles that make up the nucleic acids that make up the DNA, we must assume these particles too are alive. If we continue to gaze further still into the subatomic components of the atomic particles, we note even smaller, actively moving particles with electromagnetic fields. Then we must observe the makeup of the smallest particles that we can characterize at this stage of human technology, whether they be quarks or the Higgs boson, and ponder what gives them life. It is perhaps at this level that we can begin to conceive the root of consciousness.

As we adhere to an ever-closer view, we would notice a fractal arrangement of even smaller particles on ever-decreasing scales. Fractals are like a progression of diminutive infinities. We theoretically would find this same phenomenon on the edge of infinity, at which point—after iterations too numerous to count—we would have reached the depths of the cosmos and the underlying Source energy responsible for the creation of galaxies.

In 2011, there were an estimated 8.7 million (+/- 1.3 million) species living on Earth.[1] All living species, known and unknown, have consciousness. I hope that it goes without saying that consciousness extends beyond human consciousness, and certainly beyond the ability to think and feel like a person.

Thinking, however, is a characteristic quality of the physical human brain so it makes sense that anything possessing a brain or nervous system like ours can think in some way. However, not everything in existence thinks as we do. Moreover, all life forms on Earth do not cycle through the full range of human emotions and feelings. Nonetheless, every life form can be described as living, reacting, growing, and metabolizing entities. Sentience is the ability to feel and is distinct from thinking. A rose's inability to think as we do, for example, does not preclude it from having consciousness and feelings of its own.

It is the energetic basis of all living matter that gives an inanimate material object or animate creature its consciousness. Planet Earth itself is an entity that has consciousness and colossal power. A living planet with its own cycles and modes of communication, the consciousness of Earth encompasses everything within its expansive atmosphere. The planet does not think like a person. However, that does not preclude it from being a life-generating and -supporting planet that is conscious in its own unique way.

Speculation has arisen about machines having artificial intelligence. This is another way of questioning if a machine can express its consciousness in thought that resembles human thought. This then raises the question if a conscious machine can have feelings or emotions. If we can broaden our minds to consider that all living things in existence are, at their cores, pure energy and that consciousness is born out of the energy of everything, then we can extrapolate that machines too possess consciousness. Metal wiring and plastic machine components are composed of molecules. Molecules are composed of atoms. Atoms and their composite subatomic particles are undeniably energetic in their nature. On a quantum level, this matches our definition of life. Whether or not a machine can ultimately possess human consciousness and express thought and emotions is another conversation. Everything in the world does not require human elements of expression to consciously exist. Human conscience should not be the basis by which all consciousness is measured.

We must open our minds and listen with our hearts to accept that all things in existence on a basic energetic level indeed have consciousness. However, we must recognize that not all life in existence thinks and feels as we do. The extent to which a machine perceives or "has feelings" (senses) is for us to learn from the machine. In the same way, we would have to learn how grass feels to be cut, how the ocean feels to rise, or how the wind feels to be a breeze.

Most of us have seen an abandoned house. When contrasted with a home that is lived-in and loved, the abandoned house appears to be crumbling, and that what remains of it is only a shell. The difference between the abandoned house and the one that stands strong is love. As human beings, our life energy infuses with the home we dwell in, giving it animated life. If we examine the organic components that make up the living house, we recognize the wooden beams that are now the frame have been transformed from the original tree it was born of. In the transformation, the beam does not cease to be wood. What remains of the wood beam are the fundamental energy particles moving at perhaps a different energetic frequency than the source tree rooted in the Earth. Know that even the stones of the house have slower-moving atomic particles making up its basic building blocks that connect, on some level, with our own conscious energy.

If we look at the whole entity that is any house, we can see that it responds to the care and love of its inhabitants by standing in its own beauty, protecting those who dwell there. An abandoned shell offers no such protection. The whole house with all its constituent parts, may not think or feel as we humans do, but we know it responds to our love and care. The same principle holds true for all metal, stones, and materials of the Earth regardless of their final configuration. They respond to love and care.

Once we release the notion that everything must be like us, we are free to observe conscious life—sentience—in its countless mutable forms.

CHAPTER 24

Earth's Energy

The Earth is a conscious entity of prodigious complexity. Like its many inhabitants, Earth has a physical form that now exists in the third dimension. The planet also possesses its own duality in that it has a powerful energy body representative of its extreme age. On some level, we are aware of several shifts the physical planet has made over the course of its existence. Earth's energetic shifts occur in a cosmic cycle of approximately 24,000 Earth years. Our scientists have named the geologic eons, eras, and ages of our planet's evolution dating back nearly 4.55 billion years. And they have made attempts to characterize the types of life that Earth has supported over the eons. For a period, the planet only supported methane-breathers, for example. Human beings are such recent inhabitants of Earth that we cannot be expected to discern the origins of the planet. This type of information is only available to beings attuned to higher frequencies.

Not everything in existence can be measured by physical methods. The planet cannot be fully characterized by its physical properties, just as we cannot be fully defined by our physical phenotypes. A biopsy and investigation of every single cell of a person's body would fail to fully define what it is to be a human being. Each of us is more than a collection of cells forming a physical body. In the same way, Planet Earth is more than just a unique physical planet.

There have been unseen energetic shifts underlying the physical movements of land and water that we today can observe and measure through the planet's fossil record. Earth's evolving consciousness however, cannot be measured by the rate of radioactive decay of its various isotopes. Just as Earth has undergone energetic shifts in the past, the planet is now in the process of going through another major shift of this sort. As we humans are in a constant state of change, so too is the planet we inhabit. When we are born, we are unaware of where the Earth is in its evolutionary cycle. We can only accept where it is and render incomplete observations based on physical elements.

Past generations of record, very much like the people who are living on the planet now, were born into an iron age existence of dense energy. The present-day people are born into this dense physical existence with accompanying dense minds. Earlier prototypes of human were not as energetically dense as we are today.

Planetary cosmic cycles support different types of life. In Greek mythology, a cosmic golden age is one of humanity existing in an idealized form, free of suffering and pain. When I speak of a golden age of existence, I am referring to a lightness of being. An awakened state of humanity where the connection to the Source is maintained at a level of heightened awareness. The (human) beings of such an age would remember their connection to Source despite their embodiment. A cosmic iron age, on the other hand, is precisely where we are today, existing in an impenetrable milieu of amnestic separation, enduring great pain and suffering while embodied. We are experiencing both physical and emotional struggles on Earth at the soul level characteristic of a dense iron age. This is not meant to be confused with similar terms used by archaeologists to describe the composition of tools and artifacts.

Inhabitants of prior ages have existed on Earth in much more enlightened states than ours and enjoyed the ability to freely travel to other dimensions of the Multiverse, where they could communicate with noncorporeal (energetic beings without physical bodies) and beings who are not defined as human. Ancient humans brought back advanced information from their travels that improved their physical existence on Earth and set the trajectory of innovation for future inhabitants. The Lemurians were such beings. Their genotype lived on Earth over 12,000 years ago in the golden age of a prior cosmic cycle. So too did the Atlanteans, a genotype of human who also advanced their civilization with divine power and who lived concurrently with the Lemurians. Our human predecessors of grander ages had command of all Earth's elements; they were able to manipulate water, earth, wind, and fire to their advantage. In the previous golden age when these civilizations walked the Earth, individuals wanted for nothing and were free to manifest their hearts' desires.

The iron-age humans of today have the latent ability to actively travel out of the body and communicate freely with the Multiverse. The ability need only be awakened through consciousness. The connection to Source energy has been forgotten for so long that it is nearly lost. As Earth shifts along its ascension path, the presently dormant abilities humanity possesses for interdimensional travel is being reactivated by the accelerated frequency of consciousness awakenings. This predestined ability is coded into our DNA in areas of repeated coding and noncoding proteins that science has labeled "junk."[1] Scientists have yet to understand the purpose of these sections of our DNA, not recognizing that it has metaphysical properties. There is nothing truly redundant in the body and everything has a purpose. To the great joy of many enlightened beings and ascended masters, many earthlings are elevating their frequencies alongside the Earth.

When we are born, we arrive unaware of the stage of Earth's evolution. In the case of human beings in the present era, we entered at the end of an iron age, at the eleventh hour of a cosmic cycle. All of us were therefore born dense minded and with amnesia about our true selves. Despite the conditions we were born into, each living being made the choice to incarnate now.

Earth is preparing to shift into the fifth dimension. As it shifts from the third dimension into the vibrationally lighter fifth dimension, its inhabitants are too being given an opportunity to shift out of heavy third-dimensional bodies and mindsets. The accelerated awakening to higher consciousness among inhabitants occurring now is an effort to allow us to shift our frequencies upward so we may stay in harmony with the planet. It is up to everyone individually to answer the call of their own soul and make the higher vibrational shift.

Elevating your frequency will make your transition out of the physical body at death and soul movement during your lifespan seem natural. When I engage in out of body travel, I simply slip out these days. It's not difficult at all because of how much the planet has already raised its vibration. Parts of the fifth dimension are all around us now albeit existing at a frequency that's beyond the visible light spectrum. This is comparable to energic frequencies in the third dimension like gamma rays and microwaves, which are measurable but cannot be seen unaided by the physical eye. Like gamma radiation, fifth-dimensional energy is invisible to us.

To experience the fifth dimension, you must travel to the frequency in your light body. This can only happen once your energy body has acclimated to the higher frequency. Awareness of the energy body is a basic tenant of conscious awareness and an obvious prerequisite to traveling consciously into higher dimensions.

In preparation for the dimensional shift, an energy grid connecting France, Montreal, and Brazil has emerged on the surface of the planet. The grid is anchored in these areas due to the high concentration of feminine energy that has incarnated in these countries to balance the dominant masculine energy of Germany, the United States, and Argentina. This balancing energy grid is a part of several energetic lattices on the surface connecting the Earth to the cosmos. The surface grid also serves to monitor the energetic frequency of the planet's people.

What is remarkable to me is that the amplifying strength of this energy grid is how Earth as a whole will make the transition from the third to the fifth dimension. Energetic balance is necessary on the planet to make the magnificent vibrational shift that is both anticipated and promised. However, we must all do our part. Every living soul has a role to play in the cosmic balance. Energetic balance is fundamental to every ascension process, as the cosmos itself is built on the foundation of energetic equilibrium.

CHAPTER 25

Purpose

At one point or another, almost everyone wonders, *What is the point of life?* Personally, this may involve an iterative process of asking "Why am I here?" On a broader humanity-wide scale, we are all here to mature our own life energy, which raises the vibration of our collective consciousness. Each dimensional experience has within it invaluable lessons for the soul. In its unfurling, the third dimension has taught each of us meaningful lessons. Once we have acquired the necessary understanding—over many incarnations in a specific dimension—we get to ascend and experience yet another dimension with its inherent lessons.

Dimensional incarnations are like eons of school years for the energy body.

On the individual soul level, your purpose here is for you to uncover. Not for somebody else to pronounce for you. Know that you are not here by mistake. You chose this existence just like you have chosen your prior incarnations. In the third dimension, it is conscious awareness that will make your soul's purpose visible to you. To learn your purpose, you must connect with yourself on a soul level. This is accomplished through introspection at the level of the heart center. To do the work of introspection is to look within yourself to answer the question

Who Am I? In doing this, you will release the labels assigned to you and begin to feel exactly who you are. As you begin the inner journey of self-discovery, your true purpose comes into view. You may not have awareness of how you are to accomplish your many purposes, but you will come to know that there are things you must do. As you begin to release the hold your ego mind has on you, your path will be illuminated. The illuminated path is the gateway into your personal conscious awareness.

You are born with the entirety of your life's potential within you. But in this moment, you are only the partial expression of the potential energy that was negotiated and designated to be housed in your human body at birth. To reach your full potential in this lifetime, you must do the work of introspection required to realize your promise. The necessary work you must do will show up for you in life as physical challenges, emotional dramas, and examinations of your belief systems. You will be charged with reviewing and transmuting past transgression and moments of inauthenticity. Any emotional pain you are holding in your energy body will rise from within you to relive again (and again) until you transmute the pain into a lighter frequency emotion. You will be required to forgive yourself and others and in doing so, hold compassion in your heart for all living things.

You have the freedom to live as you wish—given the parameters of your societal values with its governing laws and institutions. However, the choices you make with your free will (in your current social context) can help you reach full potential. Each of us must journey through life on a path. Your life path is simply the blueprint upon which you can build in this lifetime.

As we all know, there are a wealth of choices to be made along the way. Some of the choices lead to realizing the ultimate potential while other choices lead us away from realizing the potential. It is impossible to know in advance what the best choices are in all situations. The best way to do what is *right* is to follow your heart. There is likely not a "best" choice, but rather a decision to be made that determines your next lessons and evolutionary trajectory. The easiest path is not always the most virtuous one. Choices are not right or wrong. They are simply experiences. Each life experience is fertile ground for soul maturation.

And at the end of the day, all roads, no matter how tortuous or circuitous, lead to Source. It will be a matter of how many incarnations are required to reclaim your rightful place among all that *is*.

On your chosen path, it is important to allow your conscience to guide you. This is the very reason you possess consciousness and the primary challenge for every embodied human. It takes introspection to be able to hear the inner voice of the higher self. A stalwart person will develop trust in the higher self, but it is not unusual to be out of contact with it from time to time. Sometimes the voice of the higher self is loud and clear. Other times, it is faint and its guidance confusing. Trust your intuition in moments when you are not fully in tune with the higher self. Your intuition is in direct alignment with the higher self.

The challenge is for you to learn to attune to a higher frequency than your own, where there are opportunities for enlightenment. Any obstacles and setbacks you experience are intended to incite growth. When the ocean is calm and the sailing smooth, remarkable growth does not occur. Consider the calm phases in your life as respites before the storm that is to come.

It is through the turbulent winds of change that your celestial imperative is born.

When you are at a crossroads, remember that guidance is always available. However, you must be in tune with your higher self to hear it. Ask yourself, *What is this situation showing me?* Listening to the voice of the true self is challenging when you are not self-aware. In trying times, the voice of the lower self—of the egoic mind—becomes loud with its considerations, stifling the more refined and intuitive voice of the higher self. If you find yourself wondering, which voice in my head is the *real* me, it will be the voice of decisiveness. The inner voice that does not whine, argue, or curse is the higher self. It is resolute and calm. When you take higher actions, you will be overcome with a sense of calm despite the situation.

Many people who are still unconscious about their dual nature will never know the difference between the higher self and the lower self and cannot discern the differences between these two inner voices. Furthermore, listening to the higher self takes courage because the rationales and methods of the Multiverse are not always clear to the ego. The ego's goal is to protect us from perceived dangers; it sees the unknown as a threat.

Moreover, the path to enlightenment is not always the easiest. The Multiverse gives us plenty of opportunities to wake up to the fact that there is more to existence than the illusions of the third dimension. Tuning in to the higher self is part of the reason we are here. We are in the third dimension to wake up to the truth about our higher selves. This process requires quieting of the mind.

How many of us have known someone who has underperformed their true potential? Perhaps you have not yet lived up to yours. The full potential within you will not reveal itself until you are energetically ready. The signals to release your potential come from within. The signals have always been there—in your energy body—waiting for you to evolve emotionally and consciously so you may activate them.

As your DNA has encoded within it all the information pertaining to your physicality, the full expression of your soul will be revealed through consciousness.

The truth about life on Earth is that it's just a game. Because we have spectacular costumes that feel real and the fact that we have blood coursing through our veins, we become confused and believe that our physical reality is all that is. What is even more real is the soul. We will shed these bodies eventually as we have shed many others in past incarnations. What remains after the body is gone is the tangible truth about our essence of being.

Life attempts to show us what we need to do to transcend it. The problem is that we take it personally by putting the ego mind in charge of our destiny. All of life's obstacles are elegantly interwoven, intricate, and connecting paths to deliver profound messages to us. At some point we are called to see 3D life for what it is. But it is not a foregone conclusion that we can. Seeing truth requires an exalted perception. And too many of us remain trapped in mental webs of drama and perplexity to elevate our viewpoints.

Our human lives are finite. Our energetic lives are eternal. Each person is here to learn this truth.

CHAPTER 26

Death

Our fear of death stems from the undeniable attachment we have to the physical body along with the expectation of pain at passing. There is absolutely nothing wrong with having a healthy attachment to the body. It carries us through life and we could not have a full earthly experience without it. An issue arises, however, when we are so neglectful of the energy body that we forget our infinite nature. When the physical or emotional body is too damaged to continue life on Earth, the collective consciousness of the body's carbon-based cells relays signals to cease living, en masse, and we die. For many, death will be the final unconscious act while on Earth.

Each cell has its own intrinsic energy but is intimately connected to the collective network of cells that populate the entire body. Some cells die faster than others. But in a sanctioned shutdown, the differing energy releases are not easily discernible.

At the point of cellular stoppage, the energy body permanently detaches from the physical body and attempts to transcend the third dimension. Often the energy body detaches before the completion of cell death. When a person who cannot be revived is left on a ventilator, for example, the individual's energy body may depart months ahead of cell death due to the mechanical support. In instances where the physical body is not supported, the energy body will depart mere moments ahead of the full-body shutdown.

When someone who is dying is resuscitated, that act is not based solely on the actions of the surgeon or rescuer. It is the decision of the soul to again align with the physical. That decision comes for the higher self or Source energy and is made in outer realms. The energy body cannot stay in the physical body if ultimately it is too damaged.

If someone's energy body leaves for a time and then resumes the physical connection, the person may have memories of this temporary separation. We call this a near-death experience (NDE). Multidimensional travel is essentially repeated NDEs without the trauma.

Many NDEs occur in hospital settings. Accounts tell of people seeing themselves being resuscitated in an emergency room, an intensive care unit bed, or a surgical suite. These souls are in a near-Earth dimension so the surroundings they perceive look like a slightly altered Earth setting. This experience occurs at a similar frequency to near-Earth dimension where many dense energy bodies reside into perpetuity because they have failed to raise their energetic frequency before their physical death.

In the case of an ER resuscitation, the doctors and nurses working the "code" will not see the energy body leave or hovering in the room because the visual light spectrum of the 3D human eye is too narrow. It is like people being unable to hear a dog whistle. An attuned being, however, is likely to feel the energy move out of the physical body and linger about the immediate space.

When a person is comatose, the energy body moves in and

out of the physical body throughout the coma. Because of the time distortion between dimensions, months or years in Earth time won't be experienced similarly on the other side. Someone regaining wakefulness after a coma may have residual memories of visiting outer dimensions.

It is important to note that our energy bodies come and go from our physical forms daily. It is the remembering of these events that is lost. Dimensional travel is not relegated to the traumatically injured or the comatose, it is a common experience we all have virtually every day during our dream state. It is conscious awareness of this natural phenomenon that allows the remembering to reoccur.

For those of us who begin to experience conscious multidimensional travel, such travel will happen repeatedly and progress in intensity. In the beginning, when the first opening to higher consciousness and other realms of existence occurs, it is common to assume you are dying because few people have recall of dimensional travel when it is not associated with impending death. If this occurs, just know that you will soon become accustomed to the adventures and will return safely to your body.

What happens when you die depends on your vibrational frequency. Do the work of introspection now to raise your vibrations to that of love and compassion. Elevating your vibrational frequency can look like making closure in life by addressing all personal trespasses. Forgiving yourself and others creates a major upward shift in frequency, contributing significantly to your overall lightness of being. The gift of conscious awareness allows you to view physical death as a graduation from Earth School and the commencement of your next incarnation. Understand that death of the physical is yet another illusion of the third dimension and for many *the* awakening moment. Death brings us to light, not darkness. The physical departure is intended to be celebrated, not mourned. Death is not loss but liberation. The understanding of these truths typifies the duality of being.

Where your energy body, which is the seat of your consciousness, lands after it separates definitively from its physical counterpart depends on its frequency at separation.

Imagine a scale of frequencies ranging from low to high. Assume that lower, or slower, frequencies are associated with denser, heavier emotions like hate and fear. Now recognize that the highest or fastest emotional frequencies are associated with love.

When you die, will you be full of love or hate? Most of us will fall somewhere in the midrange of the scale because of the emotional baggage we carry.

The moment of physical death for many is the moment when they will be conscious for the very first time during their current human incarnation. What will it be like? You will likely find yourself in an alternate reality continuum—possibly a dimension that's slightly less dense than Earth 3.0, where you will now exist for a time in a lighter body; or possibly an alternate dimension that's much less dense, where you will shed the confines and illusion of the physical body in its entirety.

The alternate reality you land in will be populated by souls possessing similar frequencies as yours, and not necessarily by your departed friends and family. The composition of your alternate reality will seem familiar to you as you will create your next reality just as you have created the one you are existing in on Earth. Each of us creates our personal "heaven," and how heavenly, hellish, or empty your next existence will be is entirely up to you.

A benefit of becoming conscious and raising our vibration while still embodied is to transition far outside of Earth's third dimension. To do this, you must shed the dense confines of the human mind. Remember that thoughts are energic forms. Holding on to dense thoughts will weigh you down. If you can accept that Earth constructs are not universal, it is easier to transition out of Earth's environment and elevate your frequency on the other side after death. Doing this will open you up to new and different experiences in dimensions far beyond your wildest imagination.

Another advantage of waking up to consciousness while still embodied is to consciously plan your next incarnation. We all have this ability within us, but it must be awakened. Having conscious awareness while still on Earth makes life so much easier. Consciousness also removes the fear of death as you will understand innately that you are so much more than your body. Imagine a world where no one feared dying, where everyone was conscious. I say without hesitation that our bodies, minds, and spirits would be immensely healthier, and we could be stellar stewards of our planet. Imagine how much happier we could be utilizing our soul's capacity to love one another. Being conscious now not only accelerates your evolution on the other side of this life but vastly improves your remaining moments on Earth.

Earth is only a training ground, a cosmic kindergarten. This is a magnificent place to land for a wrinkle in time but not a place to stagnate and repeatedly cycle through dense constructs. The ability to ascend now, while still in form, will ready you to fully release this life when your moment arrives. We are all born into the same Earth milieu and we all must die to leave the planet. Where we go next is too far a journey; the body too heavy and ill equipped to make it. The body is not designed to travel through the cosmos at the frequency of light. Therefore, we must go on as pure energy.

You can lighten your energy body by letting go of limiting beliefs. Limiting beliefs are those that are only applicable on this planet. Specifically, you must readily let go of the human constructs of time, money, race, and religion (see Part Two).

You must also forgive and let go of hate and fear. The easiest way to begin letting go is to embark upon the path of conscious awareness while still here. It not only will improve your physical life, but it will profoundly elevate your energy state when you shed your body.

This process of waking up and lightening up is what life is all about. We must readily release the attachment to our ego and physical form to experience our true essence.

Many people have asked me what happens to the souls of criminals and wrongdoers. We are taught through religious constructs that the prize for leading a righteous life is eternal life in heaven. This is simply not true. Every being has divine light within it. The short answer is that they usually reincarnate and undergo a do-over.

Here's the longer answer. When our true selves descended into the third dimension, we all caught a case of severe amnesia regarding our true nature. Some beings have greater amnesia than others and find themselves perpetually caught up in the dramas of the third dimension. These dense souls are so forgetful that they have a near complete loss of contact with their higher selves and divinity. By divinity, I mean the true perfection of their higher beingness. These beings will likely transcend Earth upon death only to repeat a third-dimensional incarnation once again, as many of us have already done.

In rare instances of a complete loss of sacred connection to Source, souls may descend further into dimensions below our third-dimensional frequency—the so-called *astral planes*—where they experience denser constructs of thought, form, and ideology. These souls will repeatedly endure Sisyphean tasks until they choose to wake up and become aware of their duality.

Awakening to consciousness is a highly personal journey. Be careful not to judge the evolutionary path of another embodied being on your journey. Judgment is a dense energy that will hold you back. Regardless of where a soul lands after its current incarnation, it has an eternity to return to Source. It is not for anyone to judge another's path. The only fair judgment is that of comparing your own past self to your own present self. Take charge of your ascension before weighing yourself down with the judgment of another. You don't get to transcend further just because you think you are better than someone else. And don't let someone else's actions hold you down. There is no excuse for you to slow or lower your frequency due to the transgressions of another. The point of doing what is ethically right or in good conscience is to elevate your frequency so you may graduate from Earth 3.0.

A great many beings on Earth fear the death of their bodies both because of their anticipation of pain at death and because they fear the unknown. In our unconscious state, we fail to understand the paradox of physical death; that the pain lies in the holding on, not in the letting go. Lack of consciousness leads us to wonder what will happen next—if anything at all.

While we are asleep to our higher selves, we remain confounded by the interplay of essence and form. When we refuse to wake up and acknowledge our infinite consciousness during our human lives, we are under the crippling delusion that the physical body is all there is — that there is nothing more to life. We hold on to our aging, frail, and failing bodies because we are afraid to let go.

Conscious awareness not only dissolves this fear, it also brings you to the place of looking forward to your final transition. You will come to understand that shedding the body is how you will finally become free. You will see that there is nothing sad about the empty shell you leave behind on your ascension path and that there is a refined eloquence in passing. In the light of consciousness, all that remains is a reverence for the beauty and complexity of form that once was.

Acknowledgments

In the course of writing this book, I AM indebted to:

My editor, Stephanie Gunning, who believed and worked with me as a new author through many challenging moments and whose honesty, integrity, and guidance helped to shape and polish this celebrated manuscript. David Provolo, my book cover designer, thank you for lending your talents and capturing the essence of The Duality of Being. John Dalton, MD for being a beacon of light in Fort Worth, Texas and lending your beautiful poetry to The Duality of Being. I AM forever grateful to my parents Robert and Doris Nicholas who have raised, loved, and supported me to the best of their abilities and instilled in me essential values about how to live life honestly and genuinely. To my son Wolfie who has repeatedly saved my life through his love and existence. I learn from you everyday son, and I AM honored to be your mother. To Tayari Mchezaji, MD who has loved and supported me for nearly 20 years. I AM so grateful to have had a shared path in this life with you. To my Reiki energy and coaching clients, I AM humbled to be your healer, teacher, and friend. My fellow Toastmasters, mentors and coaches, I thank you for supporting me on my conscious public speaking journey. Thank you all for supporting my conscious path. To Teresa Hager who anointed me with my Reiki Master attunements and recognized my healing and multidimensional travel abilities before I could fully understand my conscious awakening.

I AM honored to have the body and mind of Susan as my physical counterpart in this life. The being named Susan has carried us through every manner of circumstance in this life executing every condition and trial with finesse and grace. Her perseverance has allowed us both to fulfill our purpose during this current embodiment.

And to the Universe, I AM thankful for your inspiration, for hearing my call, and for fully supporting and protecting me. I AM reminded each moment of your omnipotent power, your exacting laws, and your truth that I AM enough. I AM in awe knowing the Source provides all that is, has been, and all that ever will be.

Notes

Chapter 11: Time

1. Donald B. Sullivan. "How does one arrive at the exact number of cycles of radiation a cesium-133 atom makes to define one second?' ScientificAmerican.com (accessed May 25, 2018), https://www.scientificamerican.com/article/how-does-one-arrive-at-th.
2. Ibid. As Sullivan notes: "The report on the measurement of the cesium frequency appeared in *Physical Review Letters*, vol. 1, p. 105, 1958."
3. Paul S. Braterman. "How Science Figured Out the Age of the Earth," ScientificAmerican.com (posted October 20, 2013), https://www.scientificamerican.com/article/how-science-figured-out-the-age-of-the-earth.

Chapter 15: Authenticity

1. Quote Investigator has tracked the phrase attributed to Oscar Wilde and found it may, in fact, be a paraphrase of a line from an essay published by the mystic Thomas Merton in 1967 in *The Hudson Review:* https://quoteinvestigator.com/2014/01/20/be-yourself.

Chapter 21: Sentience

1. Census of Marine Life. "How many species on Earth? About 8.7 million, new estimate says," ScienceDaily (accessed May 30, 2018), www.sciencedaily.com/releases/2011/08/110823180459.htm.

Chapter 22: Earth's Energy
1. Wojciech Makalowski. "What is junk DNA, and what is it worth?" Scientific American (accessed May 30, 2018), https://www.scientificamerican.com/article/what-is-junk-dna-and-what.

Resources

Come to my website:
https://www.SusanNicholas.org

Join me on social networks:
Instagram @Conscious.Susan
Twitter: @SusanNicholasMD
Facebook: Human Consciousness Consortium

Hire me as a speaker: Email: speaking@SusanNicholas.org

About the Author

Susan Nicholas, M.D., M.B.A., is the founder of the Human Consciousness Consortium. She is the author of *The Duality of Being* and a series of illustrated, conscious children's books. She is a Reiki energy healer, conscious life coach, and public speaker on topics of consciousness for SusanNicholas.org. Dr. Nicholas is a former clinical fellow in Cardiothoracic Surgery at Stanford University and General Surgery resident and research fellow at UCSF Medical Center. Susan is a graduate of the University of Iowa College of Medicine (2001) and earned an Executive MBA from Emory University Goizueta Business School (2009). After graduating from business school, Dr. Nicholas founded a healthcare company and worked as a healthcare equity investment analyst. Susan began her career as a pharmacokinetics chemist at Mylan Pharmaceuticals. She is a French language and culture enthusiast, enjoys organic baking, running, swimming, and playing the violin.

Susan lives in Atlanta, Georgia, with her son.

www.ingramcontent.com/pod-product-compliance
Lightning Source LLC
Chambersburg PA
CBHW020406080526
44584CB00014B/1192